Counseling Skills For Total Beginners

Quentin Q. Thornton

Introduction

Welcome to this book, a comprehensive resource designed to provide practical insights and techniques for individuals interested in the field of counselling. Counselling plays a crucial role in helping people navigate through challenging times, enhance their well-being, and achieve personal growth. This guide will equip you with essential knowledge and skills to effectively engage in the counselling process and make a positive impact on the lives of others.

We will begin by exploring the context of counselling, understanding why some individuals may hesitate to seek counselling and identifying common obstacles that can hinder their progress. By gaining insight into these factors, you will be better prepared to address them and create a supportive environment that encourages individuals to engage in counselling.

What exactly is counselling? We will delve into the definition, purpose, and foundations of counselling, shedding light on its historical origins and evolution. Understanding the breadth and depth of counselling will provide a solid foundation for your practice and help you communicate its value to others.

Counselling is a powerful tool that can benefit a wide range of individuals. We will explore the diverse population that can benefit from counselling, emphasizing the importance of cultural sensitivity and recognizing the unique needs and backgrounds of clients. By developing a client-centered approach, you will be able to adapt your counselling techniques to meet the specific needs of each individual.

The initial counselling session sets the stage for the therapeutic journey. We will discuss key considerations for the first session, including establishing rapport, creating a safe and confidential space, and setting clear expectations. By building trust and laying a solid foundation, you will create an environment that fosters open and honest communication.

Ethics, values, and boundaries are fundamental aspects of counselling practice. We will delve into the ethical principles that guide counselling professionals, emphasizing the importance of maintaining professional boundaries and upholding client confidentiality. Understanding these ethical considerations will ensure that your counselling practice is conducted with integrity and professionalism.

To develop effective counselling skills, we will explore essential techniques that facilitate meaningful and productive therapeutic conversations. We will start by focusing on self-awareness and self-reflection, recognizing that personal growth and introspection are integral to becoming an effective counsellor. Attentive listening, establishing relationships, and using effective questioning, exploring, clarifying, and summarizing techniques will be explored in depth. Additionally, we will emphasize the importance of affirmation, empathy, respect, and non-judgment in creating a supportive and non-threatening therapeutic environment.

We will also address the significance of finding focus and identifying steps forward in the counselling process. By helping clients explore silence, delve into their unconscious thoughts and emotions, and cultivate a sense of presence, you will guide them toward greater self-awareness and personal growth.

Throughout this guide, we will emphasize the practical application of counselling techniques. Real-life scenarios and case studies will illustrate how counselling principles can be applied in various situations. By integrating theoretical knowledge with practical skills, you will be equipped to make a positive difference in the lives of individuals seeking support and guidance.

Embark on this journey of discovery and growth as we explore the world of counselling together. By mastering the essential counselling skills and embracing the core values of the profession, you will empower individuals to overcome challenges, cultivate resilience, and lead fulfilling lives. Let us begin this practical guide to counselling and unlock the potential within yourself to make a profound impact on the well-being of others.

Contents

PART ONE: Counselling in context

1. Why people don't go for counselling (and that might include you)?

Counselling is a word that often frightens people, and if someone suggests we need counselling we either think: 'They think I'm mad' or 'I don't need their help.' Feeling that counselling is for 'mad' people or for people who cannot cope, and worrying about the stigma attached to that, is a common reason why people who could benefit from counselling sometimes don't seek help.

Listen for a moment to the experience of May, who came to see me a few years ago. She had just split up with her boyfriend, a relationship in which May had invested a great deal of herself. She had never been to counselling before, and was quite uncomfortable about the idea. 'I'm not that kind of person', she said with emphasis. 'What kinds of people go for counselling?' I gently enquired. 'You know, people who haven't got friends, sad people, oh, I don't know', May cried. I replied, 'Sometimes things happen that are too much for even our friends. We don't want to deal with their pity, shock, or "I told you so". Sometimes there is the relief of experiencing the comfort of a stranger. That's what counselling is for.' May looked up, blinked as if acknowledging that something important had just occurred and then settled back into her seat. She came back for eight more sessions of counselling which enabled her to acknowledge the pain of loss and to begin to see herself differently.

Clearly it had not been an easy decision for May to come for counselling. So why is it that many people find it difficult to see a counsellor? What stops us from going for counselling? What are the obstacles? Why can't we just take a tablet? It would be so much easier if we could complete a psychological quiz that gives us the simple answer: 'You are this kind of person and this is what you need to do.' In fact, to a certain extent we can. There are various research-led, evidence-based and reliable questionnaires used to measure key factors in mental health such as depression (Patient Health Questionnaire PHQ9), anxiety (Generalized Anxiety Disorder GAD7) and general psychological well-being and functioning (CORE-OM, a client self-report questionnaire designed to be administered before and after therapy). These tend to be used in some, but not all, formal counselling contexts rather than in the more informal opportunities where we use counselling skills. However, sometimes it can be useful to bring them into the more informal arena.

A long-standing friend, Tom, came to stay for the weekend because he was feeling depressed and wanted some 'space'. It soon became clear to me that his depression was pronounced. I would ask him a simple question, 'What would you like for dinner?' and it took him fifteen minutes to answer, with no awareness that such a length of time had gone by. As I am not medically trained I suggested he visit his GP. Tom was reluctant to do this; however, I had a PHQ9 depression questionnaire available (as I often use them with my clients), so I asked him to fill this out. This gave a measure of just how depressed he actually was and it helped Tom see this for himself. He took the form with him when he visited his GP and they also found it very helpful, as sometimes when depression hits it can be difficult to communicate fully how you are feeling. The GP offered Tom anti-depressant medication and suggested a brief course of cognitive-based support from a counsellor. Up until this point he had been resistant to my suggestion that counselling could help and had raised all sorts of objections. Tom found the cognitive therapy group very helpful in identifying and confronting the recurrent thinking patterns that triggered some aspects of his depression. The good news is that, despite being signed off work for eight weeks, Tom was able to return to work and function just as well as before. In fact, Tom being off work was helpful as his manager needed to cover

Tom's job and discovered for himself just how difficult it was, and provided more support from that point on.

Obstacles to counselling
What are the kinds of objections people raise that prevent them from going for counselling?

Obstacle 1: 'Counselling is a sign of weakness.'
This is a contemporary version of the outmoded British 'stiff upper lip' tradition that suppresses the visible display of any emotion, which is seen as a sign of weakness. In a recent television drama a central character plays the role of a counsellor but is also a volunteer with the Samaritans (an invaluable UK telephone helpline available 24/7). His partner says, 'I can't imagine what it's like, spending all day listening to people moaning at you and you still volunteer to do more. You are a good man.' The implication is that people going for counselling are just moaning. Yet even if we maintain our stiff upper lips, our emotions are still there, felt and experienced, even if not displayed, and remain 'locked up' like a prisoner waiting for a release date. In fact, far from it being 'weak' to release these emotions, it takes real strength and courage to look at problem areas and examine painful feelings. Starting counselling is often the first step in identifying difficulties and resolving problems.

Obstacle 2: 'What's wrong with talking to my friends? What does a counsellor do that they can't?'
Friends are great, especially in times of trouble. They rally round, offer support and advice even if we don't want it, and make sure we know that they care. But friends are not so great when we are just stuck or our issues don't resolve in ways others expect. Yet precisely because someone is a friend we offer them as much as they offer us. Friendship at its best is a mutual exchange of listening, sharing and caring, where we take responsibility for our friend as well as

ourselves. As May discovered, counselling offers a very different kind of relationship. In counselling you are the sole focus of the work where the counsellor uses their therapeutic skills to listen to you in your confusion and 'stuckness'. You don't need to take any responsibility for the counsellor and can therefore view your issues with more clarity.

Obstacle 3: 'I don't want to rely on anyone.'

We can become so focused on the need to be self-sufficient. We think, 'I must do this' or 'I must do that' in order to prove how strong, tough, independent or resilient we have become, and we almost begin to develop a false sense of self. On the outside we appear strong (the false self) while we are really feeling weak and vulnerable but cannot let others see this (the real self). Often this response comes from a painful experience early in life of being let down, and this is exactly an area where counselling can really help.

Obstacle 4: 'I'll be letting my family down.'

Families are always complicated, and we can often feel a sense of split loyalties. Many families or relationships operate with some form of unspoken taboo that you mustn't speak about either the family or your relationships within the family to anyone else. This 'family loyalty' is especially strong in many ethnic and some religious communities, where it extends beyond the immediate family itself. But within wider society there are problematic issues that need addressing, the discussion of which is hindered by this taboo. Sexual abuse is still a very difficult subject to acknowledge and work with, but there are many other forms abuse can take. For example, domestic abuse or intimate partner violence is far more prevalent than is commonly recognized. Yet even when people are at breaking point, physically and emotionally, their fear of telling another person and 'betraying' a loved one is overwhelming. People who need counselling often don't go for it because of feelings of shame, believing they are betraying someone, in a form of mistaken loyalty.

There is also a fear that if they talk about their past there will be consequences involving social workers or the Police, especially if there are children involved.

Obstacle 5: 'I don't want to ask for help.'
Most of us find this difficult to do. I once leapt over a pedestrian barrier, caught my foot on the top and fell directly onto my wrist, which cracked. Lying on the pavement struggling to get up I heard someone ask, 'Are you all right mate?' I replied, blinking back the tears, 'I'm fine.' A subsequent visit to casualty saw my arm encased in plaster from my shoulder to my fingertips, so clearly I was anything but fine, but due to pride and shame I wasn't able to accept help when it was both needed and offered. Psychologically people often do the same, often because it means acknowledging that there really is a problem. Underlying this fear of asking for help is another concern: that if they do acknowledge a problem, their life really will fall apart. Yet usually the opposite happens. The relief at being able to talk to another person helps reduce anxiety. Asking for help is a healthy sign of maturity and growing self-awareness. We can often begin to understand our problems better, and counselling offers a safe context to explore painful feelings and make difficult choices.

Obstacle 6: 'I don't want anyone to know.'
There are events, actions and memories in each of our lives that we don't want anyone else to know, whether because of guilt, embarrassment or shame. One common fear about counselling is, 'Who else will find out what I have said?' Counsellors use the word 'confidentiality' to explain that all information they receive about you will be treated with respect and not talked about with anyone outside of the counselling session, with the exception of their clinical supervisor (a clinical supervisor is someone who helps counsellors work to their best professional, therapeutic and psychological standards). There are legal exceptions to absolute confidentiality and these are dealt with in detail in a later chapter, but in almost all

cases a counsellor will not pass around information about you, and will go to great lengths to preserve anonymity and confidentiality for their clients.

Obstacle 7: 'I don't know what to talk about, and anyway talking doesn't really help.'

Often people know something somewhere is wrong but can't quite put it into words. One client, Jon, said to me, 'I don't know why I am here.' I replied, 'There's no hurry. Tell me a bit about you, as the difficult bit is getting started.' As Jon told me about himself he relaxed and was able to say by the end of the session that he was experiencing some very distressing nightmares that had seriously unsettled him. His fear, as we discovered later, was that he thought he would be laughed at or ridiculed. So talking to another person often does a great deal of good. Discussing issues with somebody who is attentive and not judgemental helps relieve the emotional pressure caused by keeping thoughts and feelings to ourselves. Yet counselling is so much more than just talking. Counselling enables us to understand who we really are and how we relate to those around us. Counselling often gives new insights that we were not previously aware of.

Obstacle 8: 'I can't afford counselling.'

In the UK at least, psychological support, counselling and psychotherapy (individual or group) is available free of charge through the National Health Service (NHS). This normally requires a referral from your doctor to a psychological service where you will be assessed (sometimes over the telephone) and offered different levels of help. This can include accessing a computer program or reading material, contact by email or telephone, face-to-face counselling and therapy, or support groups. It is important that we are really honest in these assessments, as we often downplay the distress we're experiencing, and as a consequence do not receive as much help as we really need. The counselling offered may be for a single session, a limited number of sessions over a few weeks or spread over months, or as a longer series of sessions lasting for several months or even years. In most other parts of the world counselling is available through voluntary groups or organisations, as well as low-cost clinics often staffed by trainees. However, counselling provision is primarily through health-care insurance. The number of sessions provided will depend on the diagnosis given and what is deemed to be appropriate. This is also affected by the level of insurance cover, as not all psychological issues are covered by all insurance policies.

Obstacle 9: 'Why burden someone else with my problems?'

We never want to feel we are a burden to someone else. We want to be wanted for who we are and seen as a person, not a problem. Sometimes we have inadvertently been given that message as we were growing up by an overworked and exhausted parent whose patience had just run out. A colleague, Sophie Campbell, expressed it particularly well when she said, 'I feel that talking my problems over with someone I don't know might lead me to hold back a lot of stuff because I wouldn't want them to be "troubled" with me or by me.'

✳ Make a list of the reasons why you would object to counselling if someone suggested that you needed it. For example, Clive, an ex-soldier, came to counselling and in the first session said, 'I don't really believe in this stuff but my friends told me I need to sort myself out.' Clive's friends were being very honest with him, although at this point he had some way to go before accepting responsibility for himself. It helps to be ruthlessly honest with ourselves before making this list. Once you've made the list, try to put yourself in the shoes of a counsellor, and come up with a list of reasons why your objections are unfounded.

So having addressed the objections people raise and the obstacles they put up (including your own), we can now examine the reasons why people should go for counselling, beginning by identifying what counselling actually is.

2. Counselling – what is it?

Entering the world of counselling for the first time can be very confusing. It's like arriving in a foreign country where everything is different and it is hard to communicate in another language. There is a world of difference between travelling to France where we know a few words from our schooldays and share a common European culture, and travelling to Japan where we have little sense of that culture, cannot read anything that makes sense and where the language is so complex we are lost for words. Yet even in Japan, if we make the effort, we can pick up a few key words or key phrases that help us settle in. This book is designed to provide those key words or phrases to help you enter and enjoy the fascinating world of counselling. Counselling can also be confusing at first because we have picked up fragments of knowledge or have our own experience to draw on, and these appear to contradict each other. It is this initial confusion and these contradictions that I want to address. Here are just some of the questions I have been asked; these may reflect your own thoughts.

- What therapy do I choose when there are so many on offer?
- Is psychotherapy better than counselling?
- What are psychological therapies and psychological therapists?
- My GP is sending me for some Cognitive Behavioural Therapy (CBT), but shouldn't I see a counsellor instead?
- Which is the best person to see; a psychiatrist, clinical psychologist, counselling psychologist or a counsellor?
- Will counselling or psychotherapy stir up terrible things from my past, and do I have to deal with these before I can move on?
- Will it make me better?
- Wasn't Freud obsessed with sex and sleeping with your mother?

So we come back to the vital question: what is counselling? While I offered a 'tweetable' definition of counselling earlier, there are a number of alternative and longer answers to this important but elusive question.

The first comes from Britain's largest and most influential counselling body, the British Association for Counselling and Psychotherapy (BACP). It represents a carefully worded definition that captures key ideas from a professional point of view. This definition (found on their website www.bacp.co.uk) states,

> 'Counselling and psychotherapy are umbrella terms that cover a range of talking therapies. They are delivered by trained practitioners who work with people over a short or long term to help them bring about effective change or enhance their wellbeing.'

In order to be comprehensive it covers a wide range of ideas, but it doesn't really tell you what counselling *is* in terms of actual experience. As I read it, it feels a little remote and not like the relational, living human encounter I believe counselling to be, and that so many people value.

So we need another answer to this question. A second response to 'What is counselling?' reflects how counselling is ordinarily understood. This answer is drawn from a range of conversations I have had with many people over the years in various different contexts. Counselling is what happens when a person seeks help or support about a specific problem or an ongoing life issue from someone they trust, but who isn't a friend, family member, colleague or line manager. While all these people can offer varying levels of support, as well as helpful or unhelpful advice, counselling is a fundamentally different kind of relationship. Counselling usually takes place over a period of time during which the person seeking help experiences the counsellor as reliable, supportive and interested in them as a person, not just in solving their problem. A key feature of counselling, and one that makes it so welcomed, is that it is non-judgemental.

Every person wants to be liked, so it is natural to seek approval and feel that we belong. Yet thinking back to your school days I imagine you can recall incidents when you were rejected, bullied or made fun of. Cruel words or comments left you feeling isolated or unaccepted. We discovered how unfair life is when we are judged, devalued, dismissed or seen as irrelevant. The negative judgements made about us seem to haunt us like hungry ghosts, consuming all the positive and good things people say about us. Now imagine how much freer you would feel about yourself and more able to communicate if all of those judgements were suddenly removed: this is the point of a counsellor.

Counsellors are able to respect clients' points of view even if they are very different from their own thoughts or feelings. We will explore just how powerful this is for the client in a later chapter.

There is a common misconception that counselling is just about giving advice, as if counsellors are experts at 'advice-giving'. But actually it's less about guidance and more about talking to somebody who listens. A client said to me recently about their mother, 'All she wants to do is give me advice. I know she cares but I don't want advice. I know she is trying to help but when I don't take up her advice she gets hurt and I feel bad again.' Counsellors accept us, don't judge and help us understand why we think or feel the way we do. Counselling gives us permission to think and feel about ourselves in new ways, with the expectation of confidentiality (an important subject we'll come back to in a later chapter). During a counselling session, you will be encouraged to express your thoughts, feelings, hopes, fears and emotions. By discussing what is important to you and what concerns you, a counsellor can help you to gain a better understanding or insight into your thinking and feeling.

Insight. This term is often used in counselling, but like any piece of jargon or shorthand way of speaking, it can be hard to know what it actually means. Insight is when we discover something or see something in a new way, as if the eyes of the mind have been opened. Freud used the term to describe what happened when a patient acknowledged the significance or severity of their issues, as if discovering them for the first time. It's the equivalent of a cartoon 'light bulb' moment. Counselling can help a person recover insight into themselves that may have been blocked in some way.

Counselling offers more than just insight. It can lead to identifying possible solutions that come from the client, rather than the counsellor. A consequence of this is that counselling by focusing on the 'self 'can greatly enhance our sense of self-worth and self-esteem.

Self

So what is this 'self' that precedes awareness, development or exploration? The word is used almost interchangeably with the term 'person', although 'self' focuses more often on the inner or psychological aspects of human make-up. The term 'self' is used so widely that most people just assume we have a 'self' as if it has always existed. Yet in the history of ideas about what it is to be human the idea of 'self' is a new kid on the block. It is important we understand this concept as it's a pivotal idea in all counselling theories and the foundation of counselling skills, as well as in our personal experience.

We start with the self of our own lives. The psychoanalyst Donald Winnicott believed that 'good enough' psychological support in early life enabled a healthy sense of self to emerge, which he called the 'true self'. This 'true self' is a unique potential in each child, existing at the core of their being, which is expressed in aliveness, creativity, and imagination. Winnicott's ideas are rather more complex than this brief summary as the 'true self' also has a mysterious quality as well. By contrast the 'false self' (not meant in a negative or dishonest way) is part of us that we develop to adapt to any context we are in, in order to protect the 'true self'. This is necessary as the 'true self' is elusive, fluid and fragile, representing as it does the deepest core of our being, psyche or soul. We live life balancing the two selves as we seek to become all that we are and have the potential to be.

Self-worth or self-esteem

Counselling has as one of its philosophical foundations the concept that there is an independent self that we can discover and continue to develop throughout life. The value we place on this self is expressed as our self-worth or self-esteem. The experience of many clients is that they have low self-esteem because of the messages they were given as they grew up. Clients recount phrases they have heard again and again until they come to believe they are true: 'You will never amount to anything'; 'You are a waste of space'; 'You are so stupid'; 'You are damaged goods'; or 'How could anyone ever love you?' Sadly, there is often still a gender bias in the messages families and society at large give to women, which explains the higher female incidence of issues to do with body image, dieting, and eating disorders such as anorexia nervosa and bulimia nervosa. There is a whole industry of self-help books that focus on developing self-esteem or overcoming a lack of self-confidence. Some are helpful, but many offer a 'quick fix', which when it doesn't work leaves the person feeling worse than before, as if it really is all their fault. If it was as easy as reading a book, people would never need to come for counselling.

Think for a moment, 'What kinds of messages were you given as you were growing up?' 'How do you think these may have shaped the person you became?' These answers to these questions can be both positive and negative. Are there negative ideas here that counselling could help you overcome?

People often come for counselling with one issue, sometimes called a 'presenting problem', but careful listening and exploring reveals that there are other important issues that lie behind this. This is entirely understandable. On a sunny day in July I was tempted by the crystal clear blue water on a deserted beach In the far north of Scotland. As I dived in I practically went into shock as it was so cold, and I lasted all of two minutes before running back, shivering, to my pile of clothes on the sand. But unlike me, clients don't dive into counselling before testing the temperature of the water. Counsellors are alert to the fact that there is usually more to come. Freud once described psychoanalysis as a form of 'underwater psychology', where the aim is to discover what is below the surface as well as what we see at face value. A counsellor helps you to identify what all of your issues are, and how you can work with these. As well as dealing with your issues for your own sake, this can also give you insight into the possible impact you can have on other people, and allow you to explore alternative ways of coping.

Martin arrived and told me he needed help with his anger. He had been advised by a colleague he trusted that it was a problem, and Martin had become particularly concerned when he heard his daughter speak to her mother (his wife) very aggressively, using exactly the same phrases he had used previously. This shocked him and made him realize that he had a problem that needed to be addressed before it caused longer term damage to others. In the course of listening to Martin I asked about his childhood, looking to see if he too had learnt such patterns. What unfolded in the next few weeks was a long history of physical, sexual and emotional abuse. Although his 'presenting problem' was anger, there were other, larger problems waiting to be revealed, but only if and when he felt safe. Martin realized that the trigger to his 'angry' verbal outbursts was when he felt helpless or powerless, as this took him back to feelings from his childhood that he had never told anyone about. This meant that the six sessions of counselling he had been expecting ran into several years. During that time Martin learnt to control his angry outbursts by beginning to talk about his feelings with his wife, and they learnt to communicate and support each other in better ways.

The form of counselling or therapy provided depends on what it is you need or what is available. The commonest is a form of cognitive-based psychological support for anxiety and depression, which in the UK is provided through a government initiative called Increasing Access to Psychological Therapies (IAPT). Note, although this is commonly thought of as counselling, at the initial level of psychological help this isn't provided by people who are trained counsellors.

More help is available through counselling based on cognitive behavioural therapy (CBT) at other points in the IAPT process. Other options may be available, although this varies hugely in different parts of the country. Rural areas tend to suffer badly as counselling is often only available in larger towns. There are voluntary agencies and charities that provide free or low-cost counselling services; however many of these are based in larger cities and are dependent on grants from government sources (local and national), as well as charitable trusts or lottery funding. One unseen impact of the economic recession is that the funds for grants have declined, ironically at a time when there is ever more need and demand for counselling.

The provision of counselling is different in every country and gets complicated when it overlaps with counselling psychology, psychotherapy or psychoanalysis. (I will explain what these terms mean in the next chapter.) In many European countries counselling or psychotherapy can only be offered by someone who has a medical or psychological qualification. In the USA, while there is a national professional body, the American Counselling Association (ACA), counsellors are required to be licensed by each State. In Australia there is no statutory certification or licensing for counsellors or psychotherapists, but the Australian Counselling Association (ACA) holds a register of counsellors that meet high professional standards. The same is true for Ireland where the Irish Association for Counselling and Psychotherapy is the largest professional body (IACP).

If you decide you want a particular form of counselling or therapy that you haven't been prescribed, or that isn't offered in your area, this usually requires payment. Some counsellors working for themselves offer the option of low-cost appointments, alongside their regular fees. If you think such fees are expensive it is important to remember that counsellors are earning a living, not doing it as a hobby. It is always important to enquire what the fees are at the start of the process.

Whatever form counselling takes, it usually offers a regular time (from 30 minutes up to an hour) and space (usually weekly) for people to talk about what is troubling them, giving the opportunity to explore difficult and complex feelings. The number of counselling sessions required varies depending on where and how the person is seeking help. In some student counselling services during peak times someone may be offered as few as two sessions, as demand far outstrips supply. Four to six sessions is the norm in the NHS, employee assistance programmes that offer psychological support (EAPs) and in some voluntary counselling organizations, although a few voluntary agencies are able to offer longer-term therapy with an increased number of sessions. Counselling is available privately for people able to pay and this can vary from as few as six sessions to as many as are required with no upper limit. One difference commonly noted between counselling and psychotherapy is that psychotherapy is done over a longer period of time, sometimes running into years, although this is not a hard and fast rule.

The third answer to the question, 'What is counselling?' is that there are particular forms of counselling that are designed to give specific support, advice or interventions. Having said earlier that counselling is not about giving advice, this is one of the contradictions we experience because there are some forms of counselling that do just that. For example, in debt counselling there is the offer of financial advice and support, with practical ways of helping a person face a huge problem that has become worse because it has been ignored. In the case of debt, people really do 'pretend' there isn't a problem, hoping somehow it will magically disappear. Financial problems may have psychological origins, but debt counselling does not normally address these. For these issues the debt counsellor is likely to recommend you go and see a trained counsellor.

Kim had multiple credit cards and would go on extravagant spending sprees, and was getting into increasingly bad debt. The debts mounted up, and when they reached over £20,000 she realized she really needed to get some help. Having taken practical advice from her debt counsellor, the counsellor then advised her to see her GP, as they had discovered during her sessions that she would swing between being very withdrawn and depressed and being very impulsive and happy (this was the mood in which she would spend money she knew she did not have). When Kim went to the GP she was diagnosed as having a bi-polar mood disorder (sometimes called manic depression), which responded well to medication, cognitive behavioural therapy (CBT) and Interpersonal Psychotherapy (IPT), which helped Kim learn new ways of relating to the important people in her life and how they coped with the impact of her issues.

Another example of this specific 'advice-giving' counselling that has grown in recent years has been the offer of genetic counselling. With the huge advances in medical research and technology, particularly in relation to DNA, we now know much more about our genetic origins, but we can also discover things about our genetic make-up that can be traumatic.

I recently received a letter from a close relative which explained that they had been tested for a specific condition and that they were found to be carriers of a genetic anomaly. As this condition may have some impact on my future health I was sent a letter outlining this and was asked to visit my GP to be tested. The letter also included the offer of genetic counselling, where someone trained in genetics could explain what the options might be both for me and for my children. A crucial part of the role of a genetic counsellor is to offer information and advice about the options available, without making a decision for the parties involved.

Genetic counsellors also possess counselling skills and have received counselling training which is allied to their genetic knowledge. A vital reason for this is that it is not just *what* you tell someone, but *how* that can make a crucial difference to their experience. Someone I know, called Peter, has a degenerative eye condition, and recalls how he discovered this. He went to see a consultant ophthalmologist who did various tests and spoke in a complex medical language that left him utterly confused. Yet he recalls with utter clarity the chilling words spoken as he was just about to leave the office, literally with his hand on the door handle. The consultant looked up and said, 'Have you ever thought about taking up braille?' Clearly genetic counsellors have an advantage in that they are trained as counsellors whose skills focus not only on what you tell someone, but how you tell them, as this may affect the rest of their lives and influence the decisions they make.

Recall a situation where someone has told you bad news in an unhelpful way. How did it leave you feeling? How would you do it differently if you were in their shoes?

An example of counselling that adopts very specific interventions can be found in relation to drugs and alcohol. Some forms of treatment include detoxing, challenging and changing cognitive thought patterns associated with the form of dependence (often using CBT), motivational interviewing that is directive in style as well as supportive counselling approaches. Working in these areas requires the use of counselling at some point, but this is allied to a wider range of skills that are beyond the scope of this book. Yet it is helpful to be aware of how the term counselling is used with different meanings in these various contexts.

The fourth answer to the question 'What is counselling?' is that counselling, and more particularly, the use of counselling skills, is often attached to a wide range of helping professions. The person using counselling skills may or may not be trained as a professional counsellor or a member of a professional organization such as BACP. Many people will have done a counselling skills course, which, while valuable in its own right, does not qualify someone as a counsellor.

I used to teach an 'Introduction to Counselling' course, and I recall one course where two of the students, Suzy and Karen, were nurses. Suzy worked in an intensive therapy unit (ITU) that provided specialist intensive care, treatment and monitoring for patients who were critically ill or with an unstable condition. Karen was a sister in charge of a large and busy renal unit. Both found that in their day-to-day contact with staff and patients, counselling skills were helpful. Suzy, because of the nature of her work, had a huge amount of contact with parents and families who were often waiting for hours and days and needed someone to talk to, to listen to their hopes and

20

fears. In an ITU tensions are always high as patients may die or not recover from operations. Sometimes patients' relationships were as 'broken' as their bodies and sitting with a relative at the bedside required considerable counselling skills. At that stage Suzy was not a trained counsellor but her counselling skills were invaluable. Suzy later undertook professional training as a counsellor.

There are many other professions which involve engaging with people on a day-to-day basis where such counselling skills are used effectively. This list includes teachers, lecturers, social workers, youth and community workers, clergy and religious leaders, lay leaders, health professionals, community volunteers … In fact, this list could go on and on as counselling skills enable us to engage in all relationships in new and helpful ways. For example, if you work as an airline pilot it's unlikely you would be able to use counselling skills in the main part of your job; however, getting on with your co-pilot and other staff could be enhanced by using the listening skills we explore in a later chapter.

In my work, where could I use counselling skills to help me in my role or to enhance the well-being of others? If not in my job, how could I develop other areas of my life to include using counselling skills?

Having set out the broad context of 'What is counselling?' let's return to BACP's definition of counselling and psychotherapy and unpack this further. There are four broad strands that provide the foundations for us to develop an understanding of counselling.

1. Counselling and psychotherapy are immensely valuable talking and listening therapies. It is genuinely good to talk, which is why 'It's good to talk' is the name of a very helpful website run by BACP to offer straightforward information about counselling.

2. Counselling and psychotherapy are best delivered by trained practitioners who belong to professional bodies such as BACP, the United Kingdom Council for Psychotherapy (UKCP), the Health Professions Council (HPC) or the British Association for Behavioural and Cognitive Psychotherapies (BABCP). Implicit in this is that counselling skills can be used by a wide range of people to good effect, but a point is reached where the work is best done by someone suitably qualified. BACP hold a national voluntary register (on behalf of the Professional Standards Authority for Health and Social Care) that lists the names of counsellors and therapists that meet key training criteria, commit themselves to ongoing professional development, work ethically and have a clear complaints and professional conduct procedure if things should go wrong. Every country has at least one professional body that focuses on counselling. Examples include: the American Counselling Association (ACA); the Australian Counselling Association (ACA); the Confederation of Scottish Counselling Agencies (COSCA); the Irish Association for Counselling and Psychotherapy (ICAP); and the Canadian Counselling and Psychotherapy Association/L'Association canadienne de counseling et de psychothérapie (CCPA-ACCP).

3. Counselling and psychotherapy can be short and long term, depending on the needs of the client and the resources available. Sadly, the demand for counselling outstrips the resources available both on the NHS and in voluntary contexts. Some psychotherapists claim psychotherapy is better than counselling because it sees clients or patients over a longer period of time. However, research on the effectiveness of counselling and psychotherapy does not indicate that the length of time is the most important factor. Some forms of counselling take longer because of the issues involved. Working with clients who have been sexually abused often takes a longer time because the degree of damage done affects so many areas, making a negative impact even decades later.

Jill was a teacher in her thirties who found that, despite a good marriage and enjoying being the mother of her only son, she began to experience intense periods of depression. This often coincided with school holidays, especially over the summer. Her GP suggested CBT, which she found helpful in dealing with some negative and critical thoughts she had about herself, but it didn't stop the depression entirely. In her mid-forties these experiences of depression and her critical view of herself became more frequent, with an increased level of despair, disturbing nightmares and suicidal thoughts. Jill was referred to a psychiatrist who provided anti-depressant medication and referred her for psychotherapy.

This took twelve months on a waiting list, but she was able to see a therapist once a week for two years. Through the gentle but challenging questioning and support of her therapist, in what Jill experienced as a safe context, she made the discovery that she had been sexually abused. The abuse had been carried out by her schoolteacher father when they went on holiday together (without her mother and brother) every summer, until Jill's periods started at the age of thirteen, which explained why her depression coincided with the holidays. Over the two years Jill's depression lessened, with occasional blips. Ten years later Jill came to see me because her father (who always denied the abuse), now elderly and in declining health, wanted to move in with her so she could take care of him, as she was the only member of her family with a large enough house. Her nightmares returned. The counselling offered enabled Jill to say 'no' to her father for the first time, and she confronted him with his abuse of her and her anger at robbing her of her childhood. In Jill's case the counselling I offered her did not cover the same ground explored during her period in therapy or replace the help given by CBT. The counselling lasted six months, during which time Jill was able to express and act on what she wanted and what was good for her health and well-being.

4. Counselling and psychotherapy aim to bring about effective change or enhanced well-being for the good of the individual and society as a whole.

Jill's case illustrates how counselling enhanced her well-being. Jill also took the decision to take early retirement and developed an interest in supporting children and families who had experienced physical, emotional and sexual abuse. While she would not call herself a counsellor, she did become a support worker to enable families to recover and establish a new life. This can only benefit society as a whole. Critics of counselling refer to it dismissively as 'navel-gazing' or 'wallowing in self-pity'. While all counselling has a reflective function that looks in detail at some aspect of each person's life, it also opens up opportunities to connect to the wider world as a healthy, functioning human being who expresses concern and empathy for others.

So counselling, like the word psychotherapy (often both referred to by the shortened term 'therapy'), is used to describe this specialized relationship where one person helps another – through their experience, skill, training and knowledge – to examine aspects of their life. This can involve looking for insight, finding meaning, resolving problems or overcoming psychological symptoms or emotions that are distressing. Psychotherapy has similar aims to counselling, but therapists might use different techniques to achieve the same end. Some psychotherapists believe that counselling and psychotherapy are very different, and each form of training results in a strong allegiance to that way of working. These 'tribal' allegiances can get in the way and I personally think it's more important to focus on what is helpful for the person seeking help, who is generally referred to as a 'client' in counselling or a 'patient' in psychotherapy.

Sprinkled throughout this book are names like psychological therapist, counselling psychology, psychotherapist and counsellor, which can often be confusing. To help us navigate around the subject of counselling, the meaning of these various names is the focus of the next chapter.

3. What's in a name?

There is widespread confusion about the different names and terms used in the helping professions that use counselling and counselling skills. In a recent trip to the USA as I was passing through security I was asked why I was visiting. I replied that I was coming to speak at a conference of psychologists and psychotherapists. The security person then said, 'What's the difference between counselling and psychotherapy?' Mindful of the queue forming behind me I gave him a very brief reply. People ask these questions because they want to know more or are confused by the subject and seek some form of clarity. People need signposts to point them in the right direction and to inform them of what to expect. Here is a list, with brief comments, of the different titles or names that are commonly used in relation to counselling. Note that there is often a great deal of overlap which adds to the complexity and confusion.

Psychoanalyst. Sigmund Freud invented the term 'psychoanalysis' to describe a revolutionary new way of working with people troubled by emotional conflicts. He did this by listening to what they said consciously, through analysing the associations they made to certain words, and unconsciously, through interpreting their dreams. This involved lying on a couch with Freud sitting at one end, out of sight of the patient, just as portrayed in many cartoons. Freud originally worked with another doctor in Vienna, Josef Breuer. In 1895 Freud and Breuer wrote about their patients, and Breuer recounted the case of a young woman called Anna O (a disguised name; her real name was Bertha Pappenheim). She described her complex symptoms and disturbing thoughts to Breuer, and the more he listened, the more her issues appeared to disappear. Anna called this experience 'chimney-sweeping', but it became known as a 'talking cure'. While Freud and Breuer parted company, Freud went on to treat patients like Anna and to develop his unique 'talking therapy' called psychoanalysis, though it should perhaps be more accurately described as a talking, listening, dreaming cure.

The unconscious was an idea Freud developed as a key part of his theories about human nature. Freud believed that dreams were the 'royal road to the unconscious', as each symbol in a dream, as well as the story the dream tells and the feelings associated with that, had an unconscious significance. The unconscious refers to a hypothetical area or region of the mind he also called the psyche that we cannot consciously access, but which has the ability to influence our actions and behaviour. An example of the unconscious at work is the way we might forget a certain date when it involves something we don't really want to do, such as visit a member of our wider family. We might not have consciously realized that the reason we didn't want to do this was because the last time it led to a furious row and an angry exchange of words, but it slips our mind because there was a part of us that didn't want to go, even if we couldn't articulate it. Freud went on to distinguish different forms of the unconscious, and these ideas form a central part of the theories found in psychodynamic counselling and psychoanalytic psychotherapy. (See further reading for more details.)

Psyche. What is the psyche? Psyche is a Greek word translated literally as 'mind', 'spirit' or 'soul' as distinct from the 'body'. Freud and Jung used it to mean the totality of a person, both conscious and unconscious, and intellectual and spiritual. It forms the first part of words used to describe areas of thought that try to understand human nature: psychiatry, psychology, psychoanalysis and psychotherapy. Psyche is often used as a summarizing term to include the whole person that exists beyond their physical body. For example, while depression can have biochemical origins in changes in our brain chemistry and can be experienced through physical symptoms, it profoundly impacts what we think, feel, do and our sense of who we are. It is, therefore, an illness of the psyche. The psyche is also often linked to an ancient concept of the 'soul' that draws on religious and spiritual ideas about what it is to be human. The soul is a dimension of a person that exists at the centre of their being, makes them come alive, and which some people believe survives death.

A **psychoanalyst** is someone who uses psychoanalytic ideas and techniques and has been through their own personal analysis. Psychoanalysis has proved to be very influential and controversial. Many of Freud's ideas have evolved or been adapted in the light of subsequent research and are still very important today. It is unlikely you would meet a psychoanalyst in an NHS setting as most work privately, primarily in London. The key professional bodies are the Institute of Psychoanalysis, home of the British Psychoanalytic Society, and the British Psychoanalytic Council. These offer different kinds of training and accreditation.

Psychiatrist. A psychiatrist is a person who has done general medical training as a doctor first, before specializing in psychiatry – the study of the mind and mental disorders, often referred to as mental illness. Their expertise is in diagnosing mental health conditions, helping patients manage their illness, aiding recovery and preventing relapse. As doctors, psychiatrists can prescribe medication and are experts in getting the right balance of medication, as drugs can work differently for each person. Most psychiatrists in the UK are employed in the NHS, although there is also psychiatric provision in private hospitals and clinics run by healthcare companies like BUPA or the Priory Group of hospitals. Psychiatry is often seen as the Cinderella of medical training and is not a popular speciality chosen by British-trained medical students. It does not have the apparent glamour of other specialities and attracts less funding. The work is often slow with difficult patient groups, where some are hostile about treatment and as a consequence can be demanding and stressful. In order to meet the current demand in the NHS the majority of psychiatrists come from overseas, but restrictions on immigration and the granting of visas have led to increasing pressures.

Following a generic training, psychiatrists specialize and are employed in one of six areas:

- General Psychiatry
- Psychiatry of Learning Disability
- Old Age Psychiatry
- Forensic Psychiatry
- Child and Adolescent Psychiatry
- Psychotherapy

All UK-trained psychiatrists do six months of psychotherapy training, and if they choose psychotherapy as their area of speciality they are termed a specialist registrar in psychotherapy. This role can lead on to becoming a consultant psychotherapist (while still being a consultant psychiatrist).

Psychiatry is based on understanding people through a medical pattern focusing on symptoms, causes, and treatment with a strongly scientific bias. This is often referred to as the 'medical' model. The professional body that represents psychiatry is the Royal College of Psychiatrists and they have a helpful and informative website on all aspects of mental health. See http://www.rcpsych.ac.uk/

Psychotherapist. The English word psychotherapy comes from two Greek words: '*psyche*' meaning breath, spirit or soul, and '*therapia*' meaning healing, cure, to care for, or to offer treatment. Psychotherapists do not normally have medical training and it is often a second career where people want to do a job that is satisfying at a personal level – even if it will never make them rich. For example, the average age of students on my training course is

39, but ranges between 24 and 60. The former professions represented include teachers, social workers, academics, nurses, occupational therapists, businesspeople, professional sportsmen, psychologists, ministers of religion, administrators, and stay-at-home parents. Training involves a combination of theory about human nature, ideas about what goes wrong, as well as ideas about growth and well-being.

Training also includes each student undergoing their own personal therapy, and learning techniques based on how to relate to, communicate with and simply be with another person. A key factor in psychotherapy is the strength of the relationship that is established between the client and the therapist. Psychotherapy can be used with individuals, groups, couples and families. The key professional body in the UK is the United Kingdom Council for Psychotherapy (UKCP), although there is overlap with some psychotherapists belonging to the British Psychoanalytic Council (BPC). Both have helpful websites that explain how they work in more detail. See http://www.psychotherapy.org.uk/ and http://www.psychoanalytic-council.org/ The BACP mentioned earlier in this book combines both counsellors and psychotherapists in its membership and has a wide range of international partners such as the ICAP, the ACA (both America and Australia) and the CCPA-ACCP to name a few.

Psychologist. Psychology is a very popular subject both with the general public and at undergraduate level at university. In general terms, psychologists seek to understand how people think, feel and behave, individually and in groups. They also seek to identify motivations that underlie behaviour, looking for general patterns that apply to all people. Psychology appeals to a scientific evidence base for its work, and sometimes claims superiority to other forms of psychological therapy as a result of this. Psychology can be applied in many areas and some specialist forms of psychology include:

- Clinical psychology
- Occupational or business psychology
- Educational psychology
- Health psychology
- Counselling psychology
- Sport and exercise psychology
- Neuropsychology
- Forensic psychology

Psychology, unlike psychiatry, is concerned with the normal functioning of the mind and includes areas such as learning, remembering and the normal psychological development of children. Within the NHS the most common type of psychologist you're likely to meet is a clinical psychologist, who aims to reduce psychological distress and improve psychological well-being. Anyone using the term 'psychologist' must be registered with the Health Professions Council (HPC), which recognizes 'practitioner' status. This ensures a commitment to professional development, ethical working and an independent complaint procedure in order to protect the public. Thekey professional body is the British Psychological Society (BPS) and this also has a helpful website. See http://www.bps.org.uk/

Psychological Therapist. We defined counselling earlier in chapter 2, and from the description of psychotherapy mentioned above there are clear similarities and significant overlaps between counselling and psychotherapy. Using both terms can be cumbersome, and the words 'therapy' or 'talking cure' are often used as a form of shorthand. The UK Department of Health commissioned the Centre for Workforce Intelligence (CfWI) to clarify what 'psychological therapies' are. Helpfully, they concluded that there is no single definition of what a psychological therapist is. Because counsellors and psychological therapists are not statutory regulated professions, it is important to focus on what standards could be expected. A person can be defined as a 'psychological therapist' if they meet certain standards including:

- To have completed one year of full-time (or equivalent part-time) psychotherapy or counselling training leading to a qualification or accreditation recognized by a professional body
- To have achieved the level of competency required by a professional body
- To be a member of a professional body, including continuing professional and personal development, regular supervision and a commitment to a code of practice or ethical framework
- To have gained supervised therapy experience as required by the professional body.

This description of the standards required to be a 'psychological therapist' provides clear information about the minimum levels expected irrespective of whether the therapist calls themself a counsellor or psychotherapist. While there are many different approaches in counselling, psychotherapy, or talking therapies (listed below) these are the basic standards required, although currently the standards expected for professional accreditation by BACP and UKCP are considerably higher than this. While there is a vast range of talking therapies they generally fit under the following categories:

- Cognitive behavioural therapies
- Psychoanalytic therapies
- Psychodynamic therapies
- Systemic and family psychotherapy
- Arts and play therapies
- Humanistic and integrative psychotherapies
- Hypnotherapy

These are the most common therapies available; however, the website www.itsgoodtotalk.org offers an A–Z list of many other therapies.

There are many similarities between a psychotherapist and a counsellor. The main difference lies in the history of each profession, rather than what they do now. While some psychotherapists claim they do something very different from counselling or offer greater depth, in reality there is little difference between the two.

Whatever the title of the person you encounter, they are committed to your health and well-being. All roles, whatever the formal title, can be enhanced by the use of the counselling skills we come to later in this book.

4. Where did counselling come from?

Counselling has two histories, one dating almost from the beginning of time and the other from the end of the 19th century. The first way to look at counselling is that, as long as there have been human beings, there has been the need to be heard, to be listened to, and to be understood. These skills were often wrapped up in other titles or became part of existing roles such as healer, wise man or wise woman, guru and priest (or other similar terms). It is so easy to forget that human beings today are very much the same as they were thousands of years ago. We laugh, cry, love, lose, hurt, break, grow, sing, create, fight, hate, care and ultimately, die. And we have historical written accounts of how people sought help from others when these things happened. For example, in the Old Testament, the Book of Job describes the tragedies that happen to one man, Job, and his family. Possibly dating from the second millennium (1000–2000) BC, this story existed first as oral history and was then written down at a later date. At one point Job debates with three friends about the meaning of all the dreadful events that have happened to him and his family. His friends begin by rallying around him, sitting in silence with him and identifying with his distress. They could be called Job's counsellors, as they are essentially offering a listening and talking cure.

Counselling has a long history and is not just an invention of the 19th and 20th centuries. People have always found ways of helping other people.

The second history of counselling is a story within a story, involving psychotherapy and psychoanalysis. The history begins with psychoanalysis and can be dated to 1895 when Sigmund Freud published a book called *Studies in Hysteria* (co-authored by Josef Breuer, who we met earlier). Even though words like 'psychology', 'psychotherapy' and 'the unconscious' already existed, as did some of the ideas that shaped Freud's thinking, he took these concepts in a new and unique direction. Following Freud's reflections on his dreams as part of his internal world and how this internal landscape shaped us in life, the ideas and practices of psychoanalysis were launched into the mainstream. They become part of popular culture in the 20th century, epitomized by the iconic image of the couch and a silent analyst sitting to one side (in Freud's case, smoking a cigar). Psychoanalytic terms such as 'the unconscious', 'transference', 'Freudian slips', 'repression', and 'defences' are now used widely in the language and ideas of our popular culture. Psychoanalysis also became hugely influential in the development of different forms of psychotherapy and psychodynamic counselling. Even person-centred counselling (which we discuss later in this chapter) was a reaction against Freud's ideas that were thought too reductive.

Stripped to its essence what Freud did was sit in a room with a client, listening carefully, helping them make sense of their distressing symptoms, discovering underlying causes related to important figures such as a parent, and identifying some underlying traumatic event. He didn't rush to diagnose a medical problem and offer a medical solution. He didn't dismiss his clients (mainly women) as hysterical and not worth listening to, as many would have done given the disadvantaged status of women in Victorian society. Freud set out some of the key ways in which counselling works, even though he developed his own ideas as psychoanalysis. But counselling retains that central feature of a relational encounter between two people, where talking and listening are central to a person's discovery of themselves.

KEY
FIGURE
Who was Freud?

Sigismund Schlomo Freud was born in 1856 into a Jewish family and grew up in Vienna. He pursued a medical and scientific career as a neurologist, but after visiting a Parisian neurologist called Jean-

Martin Charcot, who was demonstrating how to treat unusual cases of paralysis in women, Freud became intrigued by hysteria. At the same time he fell in love with Martha Bernays and, needing a secure job to get married, Freud began to see patients sent by his colleague and patron Dr Josef Breuer. After his father's death in 1896 Freud wrote that his whole past had been reawakened by this event and consequently he began to examine his dreams. He started to put together his ideas about the unconscious, how it could be understood and worked with therapeutically. A whole series of books followed, most famously the *Interpretation of Dreams* in 1900. His ideas of childhood sexuality (where sexuality is understood as a pleasure-seeking activity rather than simply a physiological genital sexual activity) and his theory of the Oedipus complex (in which men secretly desire their mothers) were viewed as scandalous. Yet some flocked to his revolutionary ideas and treatment methods, including Jung, Adler, Pfister, Rank, Abraham and Jones.

Patients would see Freud up to six times a week for an hour, lying on a couch and saying whatever came into their mind without censoring it (known as free association), as well as recalling their dreams. Freud would interpret these, giving insights into the secret desires of the patient. Such was the growth of psychoanalysis that an International Psychoanalytic Association was formed in 1910, which survived both political in-fighting when Freud and Jung went through an acrimonious split, and the inevitable traumas caused by the First World War.

Freud's thinking was always evolving as he applied his psychoanalytic ideas to many areas of life. For example, his book on religion, *The Future of an Illusion* (1927), suggests that God is an illusory father figure we believe in to grant our wishes because we cannot bear to face reality on our own. He continued researching, experimenting and practising for many years until his death in 1939, aged 83, from an overdose of morphine to relieve his constant pain caused by sixteen years of mouth cancer. Having always been a keen Anglophile, Freud spent the last year of his life in London, and

Freud's house still exists as the Freud Museum in Maresfield Gardens, near Swiss Cottage. All people named Freud in the UK are directly related to Sigmund.

So many of Freud's ideas have become part of 20th-century culture and are expressed in our language, literature, films, even advertising, that it is difficult to realize just how revolutionary his ideas were. While some of his ideas have become dated, at the time they changed the way people saw the world.

The next part of the story can be found in the traumas of the First World War, which blew society apart and directly led to the development of psychotherapy. British society was never the same after the First World War and this gave an opportunity for new social, philosophical, political and therapeutic ideas to emerge. The appalling carnage left soldiers shell-shocked and traumatized by the horrors they had endured, and with feelings of guilt over their survival. Psychiatrists working with insanity (as it was generally known then) were faced with many shell-shocked victims and very few resources to treat them. Psychotherapy evolved when psychiatrists like Bernard Hart and Hugh Crichton-Miller took Freud's ideas off the couch and put them into the shattered war-torn lives of men back from the trenches. They replaced medical or physical approaches to treating such men with this new talking cure that was able to unlock trauma. Psychotherapy slowly became established as other pioneers such as Carl Jung, initially a colleague of Freud, developed ideas about how human beings understood themselves, drawing on the past and living in the present. Psychotherapy was primarily based in London, where Crichton-Miller established the now world-famous Tavistock Clinic to offer psychotherapy to the general public.

From London, and through army psychiatrists returning to other parts of the UK, psychotherapy slowly spread across the country.

There was a similar pattern seen in other countries, though in some, such as the USA, psychotherapy and psychoanalysis became linked to the medical profession where you could only practise if you had already trained as a doctor.

What is distinctive in the development of psychotherapy is that it arose out of the need to deal with mental illness or disturbance based on a medicalized way of understanding what it is to be human. Psychotherapy was provided by people practising as psychoanalysts or psychotherapists and paid for privately until the development of the NHS in 1948. Psychotherapy is still available today through the NHS and has expanded into many different forms than the original psychoanalytically-based treatments. The key factor nowadays is what evidence can be produced to demonstrate which therapy is most effective for which conditions, and these are summarized in the National Institute of Clinical Excellence (NICE) guidelines. Roth and Fonagy have produced a helpful book, *What Works for Whom* (2006: 2nd edn), which gathers together research on the effectiveness of counselling and psychotherapy indicating which type of therapy is best or most effective for certain psychological issues.

Counselling really only entered the scene during the Second World War, when the absence of men away at war, the changing lives of women and the enduring trauma of life both on the front line and the home front led many to fear there would be massive social upheaval. The fear of the impact of rapid and overwhelming social change, especially in terms of marriage and relationship breakdown, led to the formation of the National Marriage Guidance Counselling Service. It was staffed by volunteer counsellors, few of whom were from medical or psychiatric backgrounds, and most came from the Church, social work, probation and education services. Other groups quickly emerged offering pastoral counselling relating faith to psychological insight, the most famous and influential being the Clinical Theology Association founded in 1958. Counselling was also pioneered in educational settings with the newly founded

University of Keele developing the first student psychotherapy service in 1962. By 1965 the University of Keele and University of Reading were offering counselling training helped by a number of visiting American academics who introduced person-centred or client-centred counselling (both terms mean the same thing) developed by Carl Rogers in the USA from the 1940s onwards.

Who was Rogers?

Carl Rogers was born in 1902 in a farming community in Illinois, USA. His father emphasized hard work allied to a fundamentalist and eclectic form of Christianity in their close-knit family. Carl therefore grew up with the idea that people, given the right circumstances, could achieve a great deal if they were willing to work hard. He went to university in Wisconsin, studying history and later theology at the Union Theological Seminary in New York. He first thought he would be a missionary or an ordained minister of religion, but his views broadened and he turned to psychology as a source of inspiration and guidance instead. Initially working in the area of child guidance and development, Rogers found he worked well with parents, helping them discover what they knew about their own problems rather than him diagnosing and treating them. He wanted to find a therapy that avoided the limitations of both behavioural approaches that reduced people to mechanisms, and Freudian approaches that left them subject to unconscious forces.

In 1940 he became a professor of psychology at Ohio State University, and in 1942 he published a book, *Counseling and Psychotherapy.* In 1945 he moved to become professor of psychology at Chicago University. Here he did research that formed the basis of his seminal and hugely influential book, *Client-Centred Therapy* (1951). Here Rogers explored his ideas based on 19 propositions about human nature, growth and development. His views were always evolving but retained the core principles (or conditions as Rogers called them) of 'genuineness', 'accurate empathy' and 'unconditional positive regard', that led to 'self-actualization' – the process of growing to become the people we have the potential to be. One of Rogers' enduring contributions to counselling was these core conditions, especially the concept of empathy, which we will look at in chapter 12.

Rogers was a pioneer of researching how counselling works and the results guided his ideas. He developed ideas about the potential in everyone and how this could be released so everyone reached their full ability. The ideas and techniques he developed became increasingly popular, first across America, and then throughout the rest of the world. They allowed counselling to be learnt by anyone, without the need for a specialist medical training.

Rogers introduced the idea that the person in counselling be known as the 'client', rather than the term 'patient' as normally used in psychiatry, psychoanalysis and psychotherapy. He believed that people have huge potential that can be realized if provided with the right circumstances. As his work developed and expanded it became known as 'person-centred' therapy as it focused on the person-to-person encounter and relationship.

Assume for a moment you had been given the right support and encouragement at each stage of your life. Ask yourself this question. 'What do I think I could have become?' Reflect and ask another question. 'What can I become now? What potential exists in me?'

People also began to see the potential of counselling on a larger scale. The early 1970s saw the formation of the British Association for Counselling (BAC) and the Scottish Association for Counselling (SAC), which combined the work of a number of smaller counselling agencies established in the late 1950s and early 1960s. It was a time of great optimism, when counsellors believed that by pulling resources together into one or two key organizations they could transform society by helping people develop to their full potential, and thus take an active part in society. Counselling training mushroomed in the 1980s and counselling became embedded in the public mind as something worthwhile. But counselling did have an image problem; seen as offering 'tea and sympathy' and done by well-meaning, white, middle-aged, middle-class, predominantly female volunteers. This began to change as it became widely available in schools, colleges, universities, the voluntary sector, churches and other faith communities, GP surgeries, other parts of the NHS and in the workplace. More and more books about counselling were published. Whether they helped or hindered (it depends on one's view), self-help manuals became part of this new desire to understand and improve oneself.

As a profession counselling continually evolves. For example the SAC evolved into the Confederation of Scottish Counselling Agencies (COSCA) and BAC became BACP (incorporating the word psychotherapy). This name change acknowledged that counsellors and psychotherapists wanted to be part of a united profession and BACP pursues a vision of working towards building an emotionally healthy society. It has over 40,000 members and is at the forefront of developing counselling as a profession involved in working with government agencies such as the Department of Health.

One other important development has been the evolution of cognitive-based therapies, often simply referred to as CBT, although it covers a wide range of approaches and it also is evolving all the time. Like the term counselling, CBT is an umbrella term and its origins lie in ideas about how the human mind and thought processes shape our sense of self. CBT combines three distinct but overlapping sets of theories: behaviourism, behavioural therapy and cognitive theories applied in a therapeutic context. Most people have

41

heard of Pavlov's dogs, even if they know little else about them other than the fact that you won't find them appearing at Crufts.

Pavlov was a Russian scientist in the 1920s who did an experiment on how dogs could be conditioned to respond to stimuli, especially when it led to a reward. From this he developed the idea of 'conditional reflexes'. His ideas were made widely known in Europe and the USA by another influential researcher, John Watson. The idea of 'classical conditioning' became a key concept in behaviourism. B.F. Skinner built on this, adding 'operant conditioning' where a response could be further reinforced by the consequences of either reward or punishment. These ideas explain how psychological problems that develop can be changed if the circumstances or environment that produced them is changed, especially when allied to gaining a reward for the change. The flaw in all these approaches was that they adopted a mechanical view of human nature, leaving little space for free will and seeing all behaviour as determined. While not wanting to get into a complex philosophical debate, generally this does not fit with the way most people view their lives. However, as CBT has evolved it has overcome some of these older, mechanistic ways of working and can be of value in understanding aspects of behaviour, and as a treatment when this becomes problematic.

Ian grew up in a violent family, ruled by a drunken, aggressive and abusive father. He learnt to associate anger with physical violence and so as an adult couldn't allow himself to become angry. In fact, any situation of potential confrontation caused him to become anxious and fearful: although no longer in this family the conditioned behaviour remained. Ian was sent to a cognitive therapist by the occupational health department of his organization. He was motivated to change by a desire for the promotion he both wanted and deserved. He learnt positive ways of expressing anger and was able to break the link between anger as an expression of powerful feeling and as violence. He consequently became more relaxed at work and was able to deal with conflict constructively rather than by becoming scared and withdrawing. He was also promoted.

In the 1960s Aaron Beck and Albert Ellis began to apply new ideas about how our thinking develops and influences our mental states, especially in the case of anxiety and depression. Beck developed a rating scale for depression and showed how automatic negative thoughts could be challenged, allowing people to cope with some aspects of depression in much better ways. These were developed in the UK by John Tisdale and Melanie Fennell at Oxford University and spearheaded the development of what we now call CBT. This has become the treatment of choice in the NHS as they believe there is more evidence that it is effective than exists for other forms of counselling and psychotherapy. This forms the basis of current and lively debates, as much of this evidence is disputed and sometimes evidence for the effectiveness of other therapies is overlooked.

 When we experience a psychological problem, such as a relationship break-up, what do we most need?

- An understanding about how past relationships, especially with parents or other important figures, have shaped the way we see ourselves?
- Accepting, non-judgemental friends that listen and help us find our own way through the issues?
- A way of challenging the critical thoughts we have about ourselves, our achievements and the way we feel?

Each of these potential solutions represents one of the three foundations on which counselling is built, based on the work of Freud, Rogers or cognitive therapies. Clearly each has something to offer and no one form of counselling suits everyone, as all forms of counselling contribute to health and well-being.

The next chapter helps us see more clearly what it is that counselling does when experienced in the counselling room.

5. Counselling – what does it do?

Before examining what counselling does, it is helpful to understand what counselling doesn't do. Contrary to public opinion counselling is not about giving you advice or telling you what to do. It cannot offer a 'cure'. If a counsellor did offer to cure you I would avoid them at all costs. Even if we secretly hope that a counsellor can wave a magic wand and make all our troubles disappear, this does not happen. Our adult lives are formed by a complex mixture of genetic inheritance, upbringing (social and psychological), and family dynamics that are subject to people – most notably parents – who are flawed individuals in their own right. They have their own complex histories and they regularly pass on traumas from one generation to the next. They make mistakes. They love and care. They neglect and abuse. They can be physically present and emotionally absent. They do the best with the limited emotional resources they have. Most people's lives contain events and experiences they profoundly wish they'd never had. So there is a natural part in all of us that wishes there really were a fairy godmother or a wise wizard to magic away our issues.

✴ Recall what you feel is your best memory from childhood. Allow this memory time to settle and re-experience any emotions this gives rise to. Reflect on what makes it so good. Now recall your worst memory from childhood, and if this is bearable, the feelings that emerge. What made it so bad? If these are too difficult or troubling this might be a sign that counselling could be the next step forward.

A counsellor has no magic wand or manual of easy solutions, and instead relies on patiently working through the various issues brought by the client week by week. A client once said to me, 'I know you haven't got an easy solution, but it doesn't stop me from wanting one.' Slow and painful as this work sometimes is, it is entirely possible for things to feel worse for the client before they become better; yet this struggle can also be the pathway to acceptance and healing. Counselling respects the right of each person to make their own decisions and encourages the client to be autonomous to the point where they risk taking responsibility for their own life. It doesn't judge, but offers a safe space to explore profound thoughts and feelings. It doesn't post your details or discuss you and your problems online, in tweets or on Facebook. Imagine how awful it would be if you were to read on Facebook something that you had shared in confidence with a friend, far less a counsellor. 'I saw a really interesting client today. Totally mad of course, but no wonder with her screwed-up family. Her dad is famous and on TV in … you wouldn't believe what he did …'

Counselling recognizes the vulnerability of each client seeking help, which places the counsellor in a very powerful position. So a counsellor does not take advantage of this, respecting the risks taken in revealing one's inner thoughts and feelings not spoken before. In counselling the focus is on you, the client, and not the therapist. It is not a place where the therapist talks about their life and their problems. If they did so this would be unethical and subject to possible complaint to a professional body.

Talking of taking risks, I admire people like the climber Joe Simpson, who once fell off a mountain and survived to tell the tale in his book *Touching the Void* (1988). When he retired from climbing Simpson looked back on his last ascent of the north face of the Eiger. Recorded in the book *The Beckoning Silence* (2002), this last ascent became a symbol of his life. He concluded that it is vitally important we make choices that enhance life, even with inherent risks.

The first of two tasks a mountaineer faces is to ascend to the summit of their chosen mountain, which is why mountaineers come back again and again if they do not succeed the first time. The second task is to come back safely in one piece. Well, mainly one piece, as frostbite can lead to loss of the tips of fingers and toes. Luckily counselling is not as hard as climbing a mountain and you do get to keep all your limbs. However, counselling does have many emotional peaks and valleys that are encountered in the process and it also has two main tasks. Counselling spans two peaks that at their simplest are both practical and relational. The practical element is that counselling aims to help clients to become better – however that is understood. The relational element is that counselling also aims to establish a relationship with the client. This is a much tougher task than you might initially assume, as so many past and problematic relationships litter the psyche of every client (and counsellor). But once formed, this relationship enables the client to discover more about who they are, how they feel, what they fear, what their hopes and dreams are, and to trust, especially when that trust has been broken in the past.

Abby came for counselling because she could no longer cope and felt her life had reached a 'dead end'. She was training to be a physiotherapist and despite the fact that her degree was going well she was thinking of dropping out of university. The main issue was obvious: Abby was a single parent with a six-year-old son who had been diagnosed as being on the autistic spectrum. He was becoming more and more demanding, obsessive and compulsive. Clearly counselling could not help Abby with an autistic son as this was a given, a fact of life. What it did offer her was a space to express her frustration, despair, and anger at having to see multiple professionals who seemed to have no idea what it was like living with her son. She often came away feeling depressed and that somehow it was all her fault. What helped Abby was that her counsellor admitted that they could not fully imagine what it was like for her, and applauded her courage in facing the challenges she experienced every day. This was of real value to Abby as it felt like someone, a professional, was not trying to treat the problem, but was simply listening to her and having the honesty to admit they didn't always understand. What enabled her to feel better was not the resolution of her son's difficulties, but recognition and understanding of the emotional cost and the feelings it generated in her. Abby learnt to trust that her own feelings were important and needed expressing.

Let's look at the first of these two main goals of counselling in more detail. The first aim of counselling is practical and intends to alleviate psychological distress. Counsellors often see clients with a wide range of psychological symptoms such as:

- anxiety
- depression
- feeling out of control
- a sense of being overwhelmed or at one's wits end
- a feeling of not being able to carry on with life as it is.

Clients want to gain something tangible from their experience of counselling. Counselling can help you to focus on particular difficulties, in the here and now as well as from the past. It helps you to decide how best to tackle problems which can be solved, to understand the level of resolution that is achievable and to come to terms with those which cannot, as we saw in the case of Abby. No problem is too big or too small in counselling; it is relevant if it affects your life. One client came to counselling because of his snoring and the fact that he was not sleeping well. As I enquired about his sleeping, I asked if there was anything else that was disturbing his sleep, such as dreams or nightmares. This led to exploring the return of a childhood nightmare, and the feelings that were attached to this. On the surface snoring seems a little issue, but it uncovered one of much greater significance, which could only have been reached by taking it seriously in the first place. Another client wanted to talk about the death of her baby in a cot death while she was asleep and the enduring feelings of guilt she could not escape. This issue seems to be at the other end of the spectrum from snoring, yet counselling could and did help in both cases.

Part one

Paul came to counselling because he felt trapped in his job and had lost all motivation to sell his company's product – automotive parts for the car industry. He had started to feel anxious and had experienced symptoms of panic attacks. There are many symptoms of this distressing event including a feeling your heart is beating out of control; sweating; trembling; hot flushes; nausea; dizziness; a churning stomach; a feeling that you need to go to the toilet; and a sense that something awful is just about to happen (this list is not exhaustive). By listening and taking what he said seriously, I helped Paul realize that he was not having a heart attack or going mad. When people feel listened to they are able to say more and take the risk of introducing deeper concerns. Part of that listening involved hearing about other distressing events in his life, past and present. Paul identified a link between an authoritarian father for whom he was never good enough and a new manager at work for whom he was never selling enough. The frequency of the panic attacks reduced greatly and Paul went on to challenge his manager about the way he was being treated.

The second aim of counselling is focused on creating a relationship between the counsellor and client that enables new possibilities and discoveries that validate the client's sense of self, giving insight and choice for the future. Counselling can involve talking about difficult or painful feelings, and I often explain to clients that sometimes they will feel worse before they feel better. This is where it makes a huge difference if a good relationship has been made with the counsellor.

What makes a good relationship? At its core it is about trust. In the last fifteen years I have been in three car accidents where someone has driven into the back of my car causing a sudden movement of my head forwards, then backwards. The vigorous movement damaged the ligaments and tendons in my neck with a great deal of ongoing pain. While it has become popular for anyone in a minor crash to claim compensation through insurance companies for whiplash, the pain in this case was all too real, and resulted in treatment with a physiotherapist. The treatment that was most effective, as I experienced it, was with Carolyn, a physio I really felt able to trust. The first two physiotherapists felt as if they were doing something quite mechanical, while with Carolyn it felt much more relational, and as a consequence my experience of treatment was different and I think better resolved the neck mobility issues and managed the pain. Trust is a vital core of all relationships, and our experience of the breaking of trust is so very painful. There is an irony that relationship breakdown complete with broken trust is a common reason for coming to counselling, which itself requires the formation of a relationship of trust.

Make a list of people you trust. What is it that you can think of that enables you to trust them, or them to trust you? It's not always easy to identify these reasons as sometimes it just happens naturally, but there are always reasons somewhere. Maybe they remind you of an important figure from your past that you liked and were able to trust. It could be that they are reliable; always doing what they say they will, turning up on time, treating us as worthy of respect and responding to us in the same way, all of which engender trust. It can be as simple as the way we experienced someone the first time we met. One person said recently, 'It was your eyes, which exuded calm, openness and good will. Your words were gentle, thoughtful and non-judgemental.'

Once a relationship of trust is established with a counsellor, through their ongoing help and support people gradually start to feel better, more in control of their lives, and are more able to make their own decisions. It normally takes a number of sessions before the counselling starts to make a difference, and a regular commitment is required to make the best use of the counselling available. It is important to note that we live in a world of instant solutions and quick fixes, so people come to counselling expecting something to be resolved quickly. One client was outraged that I suggested we do six sessions and then review where we would go from there if we were able to work together. He expected everything to be dealt with in two, possibly four sessions. While there are some very brief forms of counselling that focus on dealing with one very specific issue, this is not the norm, and so it is helpful to think of counselling as an investment in a longer journey rather than a long weekend to get away from it all.

Part two

Paul felt that a good relationship had been established with me as his counsellor and wanted to discover more about what kind of a person he was. He felt that there were huge gaps in his life that he didn't understand. He saw that there were emotional blocks and he was unsure how to overcome them. He was concerned that his emotional health had been neglected by his focus on achievement and targets. Most of our work focused on discovering the influence of the past and the emotions attached to this in a safe context where Paul could be vulnerable and discover his own voice, rather than feeling forever shouted over by his dead father. It was about discovering who he was and how he could change that. He wanted insight so that he could choose differently for the future.

Counsellors use different ways of achieving these aims. Some focus on the past, some the present, some on the problem and the thought processes that lie behind it, and some on the relationship itself. Inevitably all counselling draws on some aspects of each of these in providing a 'good enough' experience for the client.

Good enough. In the context of counselling this seems like a slightly unusual phrase. It was first used by a British psychoanalyst called Donald Winnicott. Winnicott developed many of his ideas from his 40-year experience as a paediatrician, observing and working with babies, children and families. He believed their external world was crucial for helping their internal world and developed psychoanalytic ideas that combined both. Winnicott believed that in order for a baby to develop a sense of self – vital for healthy human functioning – they needed the right combination of physical and emotional holding. He also noted that many mothers he saw felt pressure to be perfect in bringing up their babies, and worried if they couldn't be available for their child at all times. If a baby cries, it is comforted when it is picked up and held, but it cannot be picked up every time. Mothers are busy and have multiple demands on their time, energy and availability. Yet the memory of being comforted enables the baby to bear those times when it is not possible to be held. In addition to this if the baby, when held physically, is met with a smile, eye contact, a warm voice of welcome, and a gentle touch, it experiences an emotional connection that becomes registered in the brain's neural pathways that are significant for later emotional development. Winnicott called these subtle and significant transactions 'good enough mothering'.

Putting aside the areas of your life where you feel you never reach some unattainable standard, compose a list of where you are 'good enough', reminding yourself that 'good enough' is not being perfect. Talk about this with a friend and listen to where they believe you are 'good enough'.

Who can counselling help?

As we have seen, counselling is intended to help people deal with many wide-ranging issues by helping them engage with painful, uncomfortable feelings and emotions. This is done by providing a secure relationship in which it feels safe to talk about issues on a regular, often weekly, basis. To discover that there is a person who knows the worst about us and doesn't judge or condemn, or doesn't treat us as we have been used to by important people in our lives, can be immensely liberating. So what are the kinds of issues clients bring to counselling? The following list is not exhaustive and is based on my counselling practice over the years. It's also worth noting that there is a clear overlap between many of these issues, and while people begin with one area it often leads into covering others as well. The range of issues that can be covered depends on the amount of counselling that is available. If there are a limited number of sessions it is crucial that one central theme is identified and worked on. My brother once thought it would be interesting to dismantle a watch to see how it worked. Once he took off the back of the watch, the spring ejected from the case, uncoiled and he could never put it all together again. Why do I tell you this? In six sessions it is possible to dismantle a person's psyche, to take all the bits of their lives and put them on display without the ability to bring these parts together again. This is the one danger of the second part of this book which focuses on developing counselling skills. The use of these skills requires care. We are no help with our counselling skills if we do more harm than good.

Counselling can help people to:

- Deal with loss or bereavement. Often there are multiple losses that have not been recognized and are triggered by the current loss.
- Cope with problems in relationships – within the family of origin, the current family we are part of, with a partner, close friend or work colleague. Often it can be more than one relationship going wrong at the same time.

- Deal with relationship breakdown which raises other issues of anger, guilt, blame, depression and loss
- Cope with redundancy, a very specific but overwhelming loss
- Deal with work-related stress and increasingly, work-related bullying and harassment
- Explore issues of sexual identity and sexual infidelity
- Work on issues of abuse: physical, sexual and emotional
- Deal with feelings of anxiety or depression
- Understand themselves and their issues better, with new insights and the hope of new opportunities
- Work on issues of poor self-worth and confidence
- Develop a better understanding of other people's points of view
- Work on issues of trauma
- Process unwelcome or unexpected news, often to do with health
- Explore the kind of person they are and want to become.

This list is not exhaustive and sadly neither are the messes we can get ourselves into, nor the traumas we experience at the hands of other people. Counselling can help: as we saw before it is not the answer to everything, but it is a very good place to start.

Think about this list and your own life events. Identify one or two that caught your eye as you were reading. Take a moment to identify your thoughts and reflect on these, and then locate any feelings that are stirred up by this and note them, rather than discounting them as people often do. Do they touch you in any way even if the events you are calling to mind happened some time ago? If so, who do you think you could talk to about them? A partner? A friend? A counsellor?

So when a person turns up for counselling, what can they expect? First, it is good news if they turn up at all. Going for counselling can be anxiety-provoking the first time people experience it, and it's not surprising therefore that some people get cold feet and don't attend.

Jayne recalls her first visit to her counsellor: 'I felt a bit embarrassed. I didn't know what to say. I didn't know what the "rules" were. My counsellor seemed friendly. She had been very professional on the phone but seemed a bit warmer in real life. I liked her voice. She asked what had brought me to counselling and it felt a great relief to tell someone. The day before I did think I'd cancel it as I thought, "Why should I inflict my problems on someone else?" It all seemed so silly, so petty, but I am glad I did go as it has made all the difference.'

One colleague receives most of her referrals through a website which also offers a telephone number. Some people make appointments online and others ring up. Frequently about 25 per cent of those who have booked online don't turn up. This is because they have established no relationship with their potential counsellor, whereas those who ring up have made a connection, and nearly always attend. If you speak to someone you get a sense of a living, breathing human being that can be very reassuring. This only works if the counsellor in question is good on the phone, though. I know someone who dislikes the telephone and often responds abruptly when people ring with, 'What do you want?' Luckily he's not a counsellor, because people wouldn't turn up to his sessions if he was!

Clients will often make their first contact by telephone as they want to hear the voice of a person, and from that they often make a wide range of assumptions, consciously and unconsciously. As a potential client it is important to ask yourself the following questions. Did they sound friendly? Do I think I will like them? Do they remind me of someone? This can have both positive and negative dimensions. For example, if they remind you of a grandparent who always made time for you, this bodes well, as you unconsciously connect the two – the grandparent and the counsellor who will also make time for you. However, if their voice reminds you of a teacher at school you never got on with or who always told you off it doesn't suggest a good start, because again subconsciously you expect to be treated dismissively.

This becomes an issue with counselling that is offered through the NHS, an employee assistance programme, or a voluntary agency. There is little or no choice over who your counsellor is or the style of counselling they offer. It is unlikely there will be any contact with the counsellor before the session, so you don't know who will be sitting in the counsellor's chair. This can add to the anxiety, but sometimes if we know there is little or no choice we can manage this well. On the other hand, given that the counselling relationship is central, this is an area that is underestimated in measuring the overall success of counselling, and is a key reason why some clients don't attend after the first session.

Herein lies one of the key differences between psychodynamic counselling and cognitive approaches. In psychodynamic counselling there is great emphasis on the counselling relationship (conscious and unconscious). But such an emphasis is often neglected in cognitive approaches because their focus is on the resolution of a specific problem, often related to depression or anxiety. I know many CBT therapists will disagree with me here, yet it is one of the most distinctive aspects of the different forms of counselling – the importance given to the relationship. Person-centred counsellors adopting the ideas of Carl Rogers place even greater emphasis on the relationship that happens in the here-and-now event of counselling.

The initial session

Having arrived at the location where the counselling is to take place and got through the door into the counselling room itself, what happens next? A key task for the counsellor at this stage is to make some form of assessment about what the issue is that brings the client to counselling and how severe the problem might be. We saw in chapter 1 that some counsellors (especially in NHS contexts) use questionnaires to identify the extent of any depression or anxiety, and some use a broader-ranging questionnaire called CORE (Clinical Outcomes in Routine Evaluation) that gets the client to rate where they see their main issues by rating 34 statements. For example, say the statement is, 'Over the last week I have felt tense, anxious or nervous.' The client ticks a box to identify how true this statement is under one of these headings:

- Not at all
- Only occasionally
- Sometimes
- Often
- Most or all of the time

This questionnaire provides an overall sense of how the client sees their feelings, current state of mind and ability to cope.

   Many other counsellors do not use such tools and rely instead on the relationship that is established through allowing the client to explore this issue for themselves. The counsellor is inviting the client into a relationship of trust. How does this happen? Imagine you are sitting in that counselling chair. A good counsellor will focus on you and listen at many levels without criticising or judging. This can feel like such a relief. The counsellor may explore what you see as your main issue that brings you to counselling, and try to find out about how you currently deal with your problems. Even if you want them to tell you what to do, a good counsellor won't give you advice, as that takes away the helpful collaborative nature of counselling. For counselling to be properly effective, you need to build a safe and trusting relationship with your counsellor, although this can take more time than just the first session. In this first session there needs to be enough evidence that this is someone you can get on with and that you feel they treat you with respect. It can be the little things that count, such as remembering something you said right at the start of the session or summing you up in a way that you feel captures the essence of you. Unfortunately, this is not always the case.

Gail didn't really know what brought her to counselling. She had been sent by her friends who were concerned for her and recommended a counsellor. So she went, more to keep them happy than because of any deep-rooted desire of her own. Gail did recognize that she had some 'eating issues' but as she told her story she thought that her counsellor seemed distracted. When he repeated back what she had said he got some facts wrong and at one point called her the wrong name. He insisted she come back for more sessions. Gail was ambivalent, although honest enough to acknowledge she was ambivalent in the first place, but it was something more than that she could not quite put her finger on. Something was nagging away at her and she didn't feel at ease. At one point in her session, the counsellor had told her about other clients where he had dealt with her problem very successfully. Gail came to the conclusion that she felt she had been viewed as a problem to be solved and not as a person. She did not go back. Several years later Gail went to another counsellor, and, as she felt comfortable with that counsellor, she stayed the course. Over some months she came to realize that her 'eating issues' were a symptom of feelings she had about her body resulting from sexual abuse she had never disclosed before, and she was able to deal with these issues and move forward in a positive way.

The counsellor-client relationship is a two-way street. So what can you do if you feel that you and your counsellor are not getting on? What options do you have if you feel you are not getting the most out of your sessions? Difficult as it can appear, you could discuss this with your counsellor. This enables communication, and if there has been some form of rupture in the relationship, the possibility of repair. This needs to be your choice, as not doing anything is also a reasonable choice in this situation. Getting trapped in relationships and not being able to do anything about them can link with previous unhelpful patterns.

Sometimes the situation does not improve, or your counsellor becomes defensive, dismissive, blaming or unwilling to discuss the issue. In this case it is perfectly normal to look for another counsellor with whom you feel more at ease and with whom a different kind of relationship can be established. If you are seeing a counsellor through the NHS, such as in an IAPT service or a GP surgery, it may be possible for you to see another NHS counsellor. The only other alternative is to pay to see a counsellor privately, which restores the elements of choice and control. In my experience clients have generally found a very good service provided by counsellors, but there are also some hair-raising stories of what I would view as very poor, unprofessional and unethical practice.

I don't want to finish this chapter on a negative note, although it is important to understand what a negative counselling relationship can look like so that we can avoid it, from both sides of the equation. When practised well, however, counselling is a natural and healthy person-to-person encounter that leads to help and hope. Some important elements of this relationship are the ethics, boundaries and values it should encompass, which is what we're going to look at in the next chapter.

6. Values, ethics and boundaries in counselling

When people go to see a counsellor not only do they expect them to be professional, with the right combination of training and skill to help, but they also want them to be someone they can identify with at a personal level. Counselling, as we explored earlier in this book, is not simply about problem-solving but is a relational encounter that challenges and changes people for the better. Yet what can we rightly expect from a counsellor in terms of their beliefs and values? What kind of people are they? What do they hope for and dream about? What motivates them to be involved in this work? While we may never fully know these answers there is an expectation that they will be a certain kind of person, committed to the health and well-being of others.

Where do such ideas come from? This takes us directly into the realm of ethics. When people hear the word 'ethics' they invariably think it is about questions of 'right' or 'wrong' surrounding complex debates about such emotive topics as abortion or euthanasia. It is one of those words that can cause people to switch off, or that people think of as 'boring'. But I think ethics is an exciting subject when explained properly. Ethics points us to the fundamental values we want for ourselves and for other people to live a 'good' life. The word 'good' is not used here in a morally superior way, but comes instead from the work of two famous Greek philosophers: Plato and Aristotle. They outlined how people can best live for their own well-being and for others, and their ideals form the basis of what it is that has come to be known as 'virtue ethics'.

The ideas of virtue ethics form the foundation of most medical governing bodies around the world, but can best be illustrated by the ethical framework developed by BACP (2013):

'The fundamental values of counselling and psychotherapy include a commitment to:

- Respecting human rights and dignity
- Protecting the safety of clients
- Ensuring the integrity of practitioner-client relationships
- Enhancing the quality of professional knowledge and its application
- Alleviating personal distress and suffering
- Fostering a sense of self that is meaningful to the person(s) concerned
- Increasing personal effectiveness
- Enhancing the quality of relationships between people
- Appreciating the variety of human experience and culture
- Striving for the fair and adequate provision of counselling and psychotherapy services.'

The importance of these values is that they inform the principles we live out in our work as therapists and express with clients. They show the kind of people counsellors should aspire to be. Building on these values, there are a number of specific principles that counsellors use in their work. The actual words used seem archaic; they are retained because they have specific meaning in the history and development of ethical thinking, but they can be a bit alienating. So I'll list these same ideas, but in a more accessible way. Counselling and counsellors are passionate about caring for or helping others, aspiring to high ideals about the uniqueness of being human. They want the best for you in the often difficult circumstances that brought you to counselling. Yet counsellors are not miracle workers. The husband of a colleague is a heart surgeon and he explains carefully to each of his patients that surgery can repair or restore some heart function that will keep them alive for more years than they could have expected, but that he can't do miracles. A 50-year-old male patient subsequently sued him because he didn't end up with the heart of a 25-year-old, which was his 'fantasy' about the operation. 'I paid for a new heart' he declared, even though there was no possible way to give him one.

Counsellors do their best and this is reflected in the way they treat clients based on the following principles:

1. **Being trustworthy** (also referred to as fidelity). Learning to trust is a vital part of healthy human development and is central to all relationships. A counsellor makes an ethical commitment to being trustworthy, and this underpins all of their work.

2. **Autonomy.** Counsellors respect the client's right to be self-governing, and helping clients make their own choices is a vital part of counselling. So often clients come to counselling because they have difficult choices to make and want to find their own voice rather than be told what to do. This is a key factor in developing self-esteem.

3. **Beneficence.** A commitment to promoting the client's well-being means that each counsellor works within their area of expertise and continually reflects on their work in order to develop professionally. For example, I am sometimes asked to work in couples counselling. While there is always a desire in me to help others, and I do possess a wide range of counselling skills and experience, I am not a trained couples therapist, and so I don't think it's in the couples' best interest for me to see them. So in these cases I ask for them to be referred to someone with the appropriate training.

4. **Non-maleficence.** This means making a commitment to avoiding harm to the client though any form of sexual, financial, or emotional exploitation. This requires a counsellor to recognize that there are times when they may be unfit to practise due to illness, personal circumstances or intoxication. For example, a counsellor once came to me for clinical supervision for their work. When I asked why they had left their previous supervisor they told me he appeared to have been under the influence of alcohol, and when challenged about this, denied it was the case. The counsellor felt increasingly uncomfortable operating under such a person, and decided the ethical thing to do was to find another supervisor.

5. **Justice.** Treating all clients fairly and valuing differences in people is an important ethical commitment. It supports equality of opportunity and avoids discrimination against any people or groups. It is an area that

counsellors continue to work on throughout their careers as new challenges are always arising.

6. **Self-respect.** A good ethical counsellor respects who they are and what they do by applying the above principles to themselves as well. This avoids the danger of counsellors 'using' clients to meet their own emotional needs or falling into the trap of believing that they are a 'saviour' or 'rescuer' of others in some form of compulsive caring.

Autonomy in practice. Mary is an eighteen-year-old student who came to counselling because she found it very difficult to settle at university. This was the first time she had lived away from home. Her mother rang up the counselling service and wanted to speak to the counsellor because she was unhappy at the advice Mary was getting. Apart from the fact that the counsellor was not giving Mary advice, the counsellor told the mother that for reasons of confidentiality they could not discuss Mary with her. In the next session the counsellor mentioned this to Mary to help her work out what she wanted to do as an independent self, free from parental control, in a way that would be autonomous. The principle that people have the right to make their own decisions is important in both ethics and counselling. That is why counsellors rarely give advice but work to help the client figure out what is best for them rather than imposing their view. This is vital, as if her counsellor had told Mary she needed to break contact with her parents in order to discover her own freedom, psychologically they would have been acting just like her parents in wanting to tell Mary what to do. Instead they explored what Mary wanted to do for herself.

So given these fundamental values and ethical principles, how is it that counselling can become unethical? An area of great significance for good ethical practice is that of boundaries – both establishing clear boundaries and maintaining them.

Imagine this scene. You are sitting in your GP's waiting room when over the p.a. system you hear the following announcement: 'Will Alistair Ross go to room four to see Dr Jones about his amoebic dysentery and persistent diarrhoea picked up last week on holiday in Thailand?' How would you feel? Embarrassed? Upset? Amused? Of course the announcement could have been for something even more embarrassing, but any potential discomfort caused is because some personal information has been shared with everyone else, without permission or consent. While we have a choice about what we tell family, friends and colleagues, in this scenario a boundary has been broken. I do know of a GP surgery where they used to announce, 'Will Mrs Smith go to room three for counselling?' until the counsellor pointed out that this was not helpful for the clients she was seeing.

When we listen to other people there is an implied confidentiality and a boundary created about what we can and cannot do with that information, based on trust. More than that, one of the big differences between listening and counselling relates to boundaries. Counselling requires a physical space that is comfortable, where the other person can relax, physically and emotionally. Such a space offers privacy where others can't hear what is being said. For example, can you imagine offering counselling in an open-plan office? It would be disastrous. So we also need to be careful about where we use our counselling skills, as informality can lead to less attention being paid to boundaries. Such informal and boundary-free contexts do not mean that we cannot use our listening skills, but may limit what we would be comfortable with helping another person explore. It might be important to say to the person, 'What you are sharing feels really important, shall we find somewhere a bit more private?' One counsellor I know of used to hold counselling sessions in the garden (his counselling room was on the ground floor of the building) when the weather was good. He was challenged by other counsellors who used other rooms in the building that this was unethical because it was possible that his and his clients' conversations could be overheard. While he felt comfortable with the setup, this was something he was imposing on his clients.

As we shall see in part two of the book, even though attentive listening is not counselling, thinking about boundaries is still very important. How often have you travelled on a train and had the conversation of another person sitting in the next section of seats imposed upon you? In one loud 30-minute phone conversation I learnt all about one woman's Friday night. I learnt who got off with whom, who had drunk too much, who had been talking behind people's backs, and so the conversation went on and on. This was information I didn't want to hear and that should not have been 'shared' with all the other passengers. Clearly this person's sense of social space and appropriate boundaries was deficient. People develop a sense of their own cocooned space which doesn't register that other people exist outside of this other than their friend on the end of the phone.

Boundaries and their violation are only one form of ethical failure. The more we aspire to help others the greater the responsibility we take for their well-being, as well as our own. Counsellors work very hard at developing and maintaining boundaries and in some ways it makes it easier. When we are using counselling or listening skills informally or in other contexts that we find ourselves in, it is all the more important that we are clear about what fits where.

Make a list of what you think is unethical behaviour. If you experience any of these as a client the next action is to decide whether you wish to do anything about this. Further suggestions are made in the next section.

Nobody is perfect, and that includes counsellors and psychotherapists. We know from disciplinary cases in other highly regarded helping professions, such as medicine, that professionals do sometimes exploit their positions of trust and authority at the expense of their patients. If this is the case they are dealt with by the General Medical Council (GMC) in the UK, and people can be asked to retrain under supervision, or in the most severe cases be 'struck off' the list of doctors permitted to practise. Research into exploitation by counsellors and psychotherapists suggests that this profession is no better and no worse than other similar professions. Counsellors and psychotherapists are subject to the same list of human failings that hinder our development including greed, lust, addictions, incompetence and poor practice, misuse of power, or simply allowing personal turmoil to overwhelm good practice. This should not depress us, but neither should it be ignored or excused. Mistakes need to be acknowledged and rectified. Misconduct needs proper recognition and sanctions to prevent reoccurrence.

One word of caution. You cannot complain about a counsellor simply because you don't like them or the counselling has not given what you wanted. At times our expectations can be unrealistic (like the heart patient complaining he didn't get a new heart mentioned earlier), or it is easier to lay blame at the door of counselling when in fact it lies with other figures in our past or present relationships.

What should you do if you think a counsellor is being unethical?

- Tell your counsellor you are unhappy and why, in case it might be a misunderstanding that can be rectified easily.
- Speak to someone. If the counsellor belongs to BACP, they have a confidential helpline.
- Keep records of dates, comments, remarks or suggestions as well as copies of letters and emails that support your case.
- Make a formal complaint. In counselling services there are standard procedures for this. If the counsellor works privately and is a member of a professional body, these should have directions on their websites to show what you can do.

In the UK, all reputable counsellors should belong to a professional body such as BACP, UKCP or COSCA. There are other professional bodies in the UK that represent specific types of counselling, but those I have mentioned are the main bodies representing all types of counsellors. In other countries there exist professional bodies for counsellors that offer the same level of professional standing as does the BACP in the UK. For example in the USA this could be the ACA, in Ireland the IACP, or Australia the ACA (same initials but a different professional body). BACP holds an accredited voluntary register of counsellors on behalf of a body called the Professional Standards Authority for Health and Social Care, which is accountable to the UK Parliament. This register sets out the standards that can reasonably be expected of counsellors. Being on the register also requires counsellors to commit themselves to continuing professional development, thus keeping them up-to-date with skills and developments in their field. The register also has a clear, accessible and confidential complaints procedure in order to serve and protect the public.

Historically the majority of complaints dealt with by BACP before this voluntary register was in place involved breaches of confidentiality, breaking of agreements contracted at the start of psychotherapy, working beyond the level of practitioner's counselling competence, bringing the profession into disrepute and unresolved issues about finishing counselling. There were also a smaller number of issues relating to financial or sexual malpractice, which resulted in the person being removed from the professional body, sometimes followed by civil or criminal prosecution.

However, all of these occurrences are extremely rare, and the overriding message I want to get across in this chapter is the incredible vision most counsellors have for pursuing the well-being of others through the values and principles to which they commit themselves. BACP have identified the following personal, moral and virtuous qualities for counsellors. These include:

- Empathy
- Sincerity
- Integrity

- Resilience
- Respect
- Humility
- Competence
- Fairness
- Wisdom
- Courage

If this list looks idealistic to you think for a moment, 'Would I want any of these qualities to be missing in a therapist I may end up disclosing my deepest fears, worst nightmares, fragile self-image, and hopeful dreams to?'

✳ Ethics is exciting. The values and principles that we believe in shape the ways in which we can be involved with others for their well-being as well as our own. Looking at the list of qualities above, which ones do you think you are strongest on? And which ones could you stand to think about a little more? Whether you are a counsellor or a client, keeping these in mind can make all the difference in positive communication.

It is in this context that we now turn to part two to see how we can all develop a range of counselling skills that can help others.

PART TWO: Counselling skills in practice

Welcome to part two! I am delighted you have made it so far, as we now turn to what you can do to develop your counselling skills. If you are starting here because you like a practical approach and prefer to learn skills first, you may need to refer back to some sections in part one for fuller explanations of some of the ideas touched upon here.

If you have ever played competitive sport, spent a day working in the garden, finished a hard day at work, come back from a day's walking or some other strenuous activity there is nothing more enjoyable and luxurious than lying and soaking your tired muscles in a warm bath. Your whole body relaxes and you might even become so calm that you fall asleep. Counselling offers the psychological equivalent of a warm bath, by relaxing and attending to the bruised parts of our psyche or soul.

Yet there is another important dimension to counselling that is just as essential, and is anything but relaxing. Let me illustrate this by describing a painful event from my past. I once crashed my motorbike in the early hours of the morning and ended up being flung across a wide gravel surface that formed the entrance to a garden centre. I was briefly unconscious and was taken to the casualty department of a local hospital by a complete stranger who found me wandering along the road, bleeding and confused. I was treated by someone I initially assumed to be a friendly nurse. Then she cut open my trousers saying, 'This may hurt a little' as another nurse clamped my leg so she could use what looked like a scrubbing brush to remove the gravel embedded in my knee and a pair of tweezers to remove gravel from my face. I nearly passed out with the pain and my friendly opinion of the nurse vanished instantly. Afterwards she explained that it was essential to clean the wound thoroughly and stop any infection. Counselling can feel every bit as tough as having a wound cleaned, however painful and necessary it is. It serves the same essential function of allowing a psychological wound to heal in the expectation of preventing further damage. How can we learn counselling skills to be with people, to help them either relax into a supportive relationship or face the pain of cleaning a psychological wound? This is the central focus in part two of this book. I hope you feel ready for this exciting challenge.

We begin with the luxury of being listened to, which is enormously significant in a noisy, sound-polluted world where it is often difficult to hear one's own voice. There is an almost constant refrain that people don't believe they are being listened to, and we so often feel ignored. Back in 1989 a tragedy took place at a football match between Liverpool and Nottingham Forrest when a stand collapsed at Hillsborough stadium in Sheffield. Ninety-six football supporters were killed in the ensuing crush, and in the aftermath the police and the *Sun* newspaper blamed the Liverpool supporters. The families of the bereaved, alongside the 766 fans who were also injured, believed an injustice had taken place and that they were not being listened to. The significance of the inquiry by the Hillsborough Independent Panel, over 20 years later, was that the voices of the tragically bereaved relatives were finally being heard. People were listened to and vindicated, and could finally begin to come to terms with the tragedy. A colleague was at that match and escaped injury but recalls the horror and confusion and still feels the need to talk about these traumatic events. He still needs to be listened to, especially as this subject reappears in the news.

At the other end of the spectrum, and far less traumatic, is the importance of listening to people in ordinary life. Children as they grow up need to be listened to. At the end of a school day or a holiday they want to tell you all their news and the antics they have got up to, as they want you to share in the excitement of their day. Children often don't have the same sort of filters and boundaries in their conversations that adults do: I was visiting a friend and we went to collect his ten-year-old daughter from school. Lucy had just had a sex education talk and wanted to talk all about it. Seeing me, she said to her dad, 'Does he know about sex?' and then proceeded to tell us everything as we walked home, complete with some hilarious additions. Our job was simply to listen. Children want you to listen, and some parents say that they miss this when their children become teenagers and stop communicating in an open and spontaneous way. Of course, adolescents really do need to be listened to as well; it just becomes a bit trickier to work out how they communicate and to let them take the initiative in this process.

7. Starting with the self

The kind of listening we're going to focus on here is called attentive listening. Attentive listening offers a different quality of attention than that found in ordinary listening processes. Talking to another person, who listens attentively and gives us space to speak our inner thoughts out loud, can be revelatory. It's as if we become a more three-dimensional person, and time and again we experience profound feelings that we didn't know were there. It can feel as if these powerful feelings, thoughts and ideas were floating just below the surface of consciousness, and someone has caught hold of them for us. Allowing them to be formed into words and articulated gives them new life, and affords us fresh insight into ourselves. Attentive listening is the starting place for most theories of counselling, and the following chapters focus on different techniques that are used to bring about the radical support, help, insights and healing these skills can offer.

There is a crucial process we must go through before we attempt to listen to others, and that is to begin to listen to ourselves, a technique that is often referred to as self-awareness or self-exploration. As Fanny Price says in Jane Austen's *Mansfield Park*, 'We have all a better guide in ourselves, if we would attend to it, than any other person can be.' So the self is where we start from.

✳ Make a list. The three things I like about myself are:

1.

2.

3.

You might find this more difficult to do than you think. In part this is because we have often been given negative messages about what we can't do, or someone has listed our faults and failings. An academic colleague told me that his mother and father never once encouraged him. He came from a working class background and was the first person in his extended family to go to university. They didn't want him to get 'above himself'. They were, he felt, very proud, but not able to demonstrate this in words of approval. Despite being a highly regarded researcher he continually doubted his abilities and never felt good enough. Feeling good about yourself is a vital place to start, as it means you know you have something to offer to another person. If I go to a gym and employ a personal trainer I'm not going to choose somebody who is overweight, smokes, and doesn't do any exercise. I expect to see somebody who has fitness and a belief they have something to give to me. Being a desirable counsellor is not just a question of academic expertise or having a high-profile job, it is about beginning to be comfortable with ourselves and that there are good aspects of who we are. This forms an impression that others can sense and want to be engaged with.

If you had to describe yourself to somebody else, what would you list as being distinctive about you? This is an exercise I often do when training therapists. I'll say, 'Today's subject is [insert name], and before we discuss this person in detail I would like you to shout out what this person means to you and I'll write them up on the flip chart.' What do you think would go on the flip chart if you were the subject? What would your family, friends and colleagues say about you? Are these qualities unique to you? Would you describe them as aspects of your true self? It's important to understand how you are of worth and value to yourself, as well as to others. It is this valuing of self that enables us to believe we have something to contribute to others. As we acquire the counselling skills described in this book we are in a position to help others experience acceptance, growth and well-being. It always helps if we have done this work on ourselves in the first place.

So if 'self' is a recent idea, where did it come from? It was given a particular shape through the work of Hegel. Georg Hegel (1770–1831) was a philosopher based in Berlin. He came up with many significant concepts that shaped the thinking of Karl Marx and provoked a reaction from Søren Kierkegaard, both hugely influential in shaping 20th-century philosophical thinking. Hegel saw the human personality existing in, and developing from, a complex matrix of relationships, groups, societies, cultures, language and ideas – out of which emerged the capacity for self-consciousness and self-reflection. In order to think of oneself as a person we need to be able to say we are an 'I', not an 'it' or a 'thing'. 'I want' is a phrase we learn as young children, sometimes accompanied by screaming tantrums when this 'I want' doesn't happen. At that moment the child is so focused on what their 'I' wants that not getting it overwhelms their emotions and they unleash these frustrations on the unsuspecting world and highly embarrassed parents or grandparents. I was visiting a family in their home when their three-year-old, Amy, wandered in and demanded a chocolate biscuit that was on the coffee table in front of us. Her mum Caroline said to her, 'What's the magic word?' hoping to impress any visitor with her child's good manners. Amy looked Caroline directly in the eyes and said emphatically, 'Now!' Clearly Amy had developed that sense of self and was an 'I' who made her unique presence felt.

So the term 'self' is used to cover:

- one's whole being, body, mind and spirit/psyche/soul in the external world
- a subjective sense of self as an 'I'
- a complex association of ideas about who we are in our inner world
- an idealistic, hopeful thought about who we might become
- an awareness of a core personal being that shapes all experience, actions, and reactions.

It sounds more complex than it is, but it is vital we understand this as it shaped all counselling and psychotherapy in the 20th century. Who we see ourselves to be, our ability to be self-conscious and self-aware gets worked out in every relationship we have ever had and will ever have.

Recall an event where you suddenly became aware of yourself. These may be moments of embarrassment, more positive moments of acceptance, or even a combination of the two. For example, Sue was very tall, taller than many boys her age, and she felt very self-conscious of her height. When she went to a new school she recalls looking across everyone at assembly for the first time and there, at the other end of the row, was another girl the same height as her. She and Becky became best friends, and, encouraged by each other, became less self-conscious and began to enjoy who and what they were, including their height. So thinking about your experience of becoming aware of yourself, what did you think and feel? Just in case you have not thought of a positive experience, try this again and recall an event or an experience when you did become aware of something good about yourself.

So we must always come to listen to others with a sense of self already in place. To get further insight into ourselves we can ask ourselves the following questions:

- How do I normally give feedback to other people, if I give feedback at all?
- Is it ever constructive to give 'constructive criticism'?
- What has been the most effective feedback I have received? Can I work out why this was the case?
- Do I find it easy to locate my feelings? If not, where do I put them and what do I do with them?
- What might be my personal motivations for helping other people?

- Are there some areas I know I am oversensitive about?
- How do I deal with issues when someone raises something that conflicts with my beliefs and values?
- Do I like sorting out other people's problems and coming up with constructive solutions?
- What does it feel like when I am told what to do?
- How easily do I cope with change and how often do I expect others to change, rather than me?

When answering these questions it's important to be ruthlessly honest. You can do this exercise by yourself, but it would also be good to do this with a good friend, asking them to offer their insight into you. Note where you agree and where you disagree. Your answers to these questions alongside your friend's will give you glimpses into aspects of your personality that you know and are comfortable with, that you know and are uncomfortable with and so keep hidden from others, that can be seen by others more clearly than by you, and those aspects of yourself that remain hidden but have the potential to emerge in all future relationships.

✳ This exercise might sound a bit morbid, but imagine you have died and your funeral is taking place. On such occasions it is customary for someone who knew them well enough to pay tribute to the deceased by telling the audience highlights of their life, and more importantly, things about their character that will be missed. Write down what you would like them to say about you. As soon as we try to do this exercise we can always think of a whole range of things we would *not* like to be said about us, but hold those to one side, and focus on the positive for the moment. Part of the skill of self-awareness is an ability to see both the positive and negative in ourselves and to hold the two in a realistic balance. If we can only think of the positive we might be repressing the negative or simply be narcissistic. If we can only think of the negative we might be depressed or struggling with our self-esteem (see chapter 2 in part one).

Narcissism. The term 'narcissism' is increasingly used in ordinary conversation, but what does it mean? It comes from the Ancient Greek myth of Narcissus, a hunter famed for his beauty who fell in love with his own reflection, and so a person who is narcissistic is primarily in love with themselves. It is normally used as a negative term that covers a range of behaviours including: excessive pride; self-preoccupation; a sense of entitlement; and grandiosity. A narcissistic person can often unknowingly exploit others, finds it hard to make good friends and can only really communicate when they are talking about themselves.

Freud highlighted the importance of self-awareness when he said of potential psychoanalysts, 'Where and how is the poor wretch to acquire the ideal qualifications which he will need in his profession? The answer is in an analysis of himself.' This applies equally to psychotherapy, counselling and listening. Understanding the 'self' becomes vital for the use and development of counselling skills, as it provides the foundation from which we engage with others. It enables us to learn to listen in depth and to listen more attentively, as we shall now explore in detail in the next chapter.

8. Attentive listening

My GP, Kay, often had long queues of people to see her. She always overran her time-slots and if I ever went to see her I would take a book to read while I waited. Her lateness infuriated some of the more traditional doctors in the practice. One colleague said to her in exasperation, 'You'll become a much better doctor when you stop listening to patients.' It seems he was bothered by the queues leaving the impression that this was an inefficient surgery, though I suspect that some envy at her popularity may also have been in evidence. The reason why Kay was so well liked as a doctor was that she listened; people felt they could say things to her and be heard as a person rather than as a problem or an illness to be diagnosed and 'fixed'. Listening does something very important to our sense of who we are. We feel valued, understood, liked, wanted, significant, as if we matter to someone. If there is just one counselling skill you take away from this book this should be it: attentive listening is the Olympic gold medal of all helping skills.

✳ Find a friend you can do this exercise with. Get them to talk about something that is important to them for five minutes. Try not to interrupt, other than to show you are listening by brief verbal prompts, such as 'hmm, yes... oh, I see', etc. Don't take notes but record the conversation (most laptop computers, tablets, iPads and mobile phones have built-in recording facilities). At the end of the five minutes write down what you remember from all that your friend has said. Now listen to the recorded conversation and see how much you missed and how much you didn't listen to.

Listening is a skill that can be learnt but the first step is a mental one – we have to decide we want to listen to the other person. We get so used to 'zoning out' or filtering what we hear that we can often just be listening for what we want to hear, or are waiting for a gap in the conversation so we can get in with what we want to say. Attentive listening has, as its name suggests, a quality of attention about it. It is intentional and does not come about by accident.

👤   I once had a disagreement with my colleague Jim, who felt he should have been considered for a new role in a voluntary organization. He was unhappy and came to see me, where he told me bluntly that I was treating him like the previous manager, who 'never listened either'. I had only met Jim once before and in that conversation he had told me several important things about himself. I relayed these back to Jim and said that given the list of his existing commitments I thought he would be overstretched if he were to take on even more. He was amazed that I had heard him and was able to recall the majority of things he had said previously. On reflection, Jim came to see that I had made a good decision and he subsequently became a very supportive colleague. He felt he mattered to someone, and that by being listened to he was more able to get on and fulfil his role using the full range of his abilities. Jim did get the role he wanted about a year later after deciding what his priorities were and rearranging the balance of his life.

People invariably communicate on a number of different levels simultaneously. Attentive listening as a counselling skill picks up information from these different levels and communicates them back to the person, although not all in one go, as this would be too overwhelming. People often don't realize just how much they communicate, and so attentive listening is a means of using what has been said and not said, offered back in a supportive and therapeutic way.

The first level of communication and the basis of attentive listening is paying attention to the content of what the person has said. Note that this is not what we think, imagine or expect the person to say; rather it is what they actually said. Attentiveness requires concentration on our part as we pay specific attention to what is being said, offering undivided attention, without interrupting. It is very easy to be seen to be listening when in fact our mind has wandered far away, thinking about holidays, shopping or work on our desk that needs doing before we can go home etc. Most professionals engaged with meeting people as part of their role have developed this listening as a surface skill, like a veneer, but I think deep down the person speaking to them knows this at some level. I often attend social functions because of my job and am used to mixing with people from many different academic backgrounds. In the swirling social cocktail of drinks before dinner it is common to experience people who are talking to you, but actively looking elsewhere to see if they can see someone else they might know or someone more influential or important. It leaves me feeling that I am uninteresting or insignificant. The embarrassing thing is that I occasionally do the same. That is why when you are listened to, and when there is a real interest and engagement shown in all aspects of your story, it makes a great impact on you. Someone said to me recently in amazement, 'My God, you really listened' when they had been talking about the death of a partner whose name I brought up in later conversation. My attentiveness meant that I had realized the importance of that name, and when I used it later it was clearly helpful for the person I was listening to.

This skill is hugely important when it comes to issues of bereavement and loss. Many people shy away from talking about death, and this leaves bereaved people feeling they have no one to talk to and no place to turn. While there are valuable bereavement support organizations, such as CRUSE, which offers supportive listening and counselling, people will often seek to talk about loss in ordinary contexts or relationships. What they need is an attentive listener who remembers what has been said, including the details such as a person's name. It is easier to remember and recall what has been said by listening well, and not speaking until the right moment. It takes time to learn when that right moment is, but waiting attentively is a good place to start.

Think for a moment about the people you know and identify someone who has experienced bereavement or a major loss, such as serious illness, being made redundant, children leaving home, divorce or relationship breakdown and so the list goes on. When they have tried to talk about this to you, how did you respond? Did you make It easy for them to talk or did you change the subject? Changing the subject is a common tactic that we employ without thinking when someone touches on a difficult area. Worse still is the collusion of silence, as this can make the person feel guilty about being upset and bringing it up in the first place.

The second level to attentive listening focuses on the feelings (expressed or unexpressed) associated with the words that you have been listening to. The way something is said makes a huge difference. Words when spoken have a powerful impact on us and resonate at many levels through the form of language, the associations we make, the memories that get stirred and the tone of the communication. Listen to yourself and reflect on how you might feel if you were experiencing the scenario that has just been described to you. Identifying our own feelings is helpful because it means we can use them as a guide to what the other person might, note might, be feeling. This needs to be tentatively checked out with the other person. On the other hand, if we are experiencing strong or powerful feelings because of the subject or because something is being stirred in us, it is important to hold these to one side so we don't assume they are the same feelings experienced by the person we are listening to.

People can be afraid of their emotions and so they often leave them unexpressed, yet their echo can be heard in everyday conversation. Listening to a person's feelings gives us a clue as to what is really going on inside their mind. We have to be on the lookout for non-verbal communication, and this form of communication is all around us if we listen out for it. It's one way of identifying submerged feelings or hidden emotions. Non-verbal communication can include posture, facial expressions, gestures and the way they hold their body. Tone of voice is also another indicator, as are laughter, smiles, tears and other physiological responses such as blushing. All these things communicate what might be going on inside the mind of the person we are listening to. When someone expresses a feeling it can resonate in us and inform us as to what may be going on, enabling us to listen in depth to what lies just below the surface. For example, research has revealed that if a person wants to know whether another person likes them, they rely on what they say (10 per cent), their tone of voice (40 per cent) and facial clues, such as a smiling or eye contact (50 per cent).

✳   Find a partner to practise with. Think of the food/drink you most dislike. In my case it's coffee, even in its mildest form in coffee cake. I even dislike the smell. Now say to your partner, 'My absolutely favourite food/drink in the world is [insert food you hate]'. Ask your partner what they saw and heard when you made this statement. Were they convinced? Was there a contradiction between what you said and how you said it? Try to discover if there were any clues you unknowingly gave away that were noted by the other person. They might have picked these up without even realizing what they were doing, so it is important to identify what these were.

🎙   Linda, a head teacher in a very busy school, told me that everything was going fine. I asked how she felt because she had communicated to me, by her tone of voice and the way she held her body, that she seemed to be carrying the weight of the world on her shoulders. As it turned out, Linda was feeling overwhelmed by the enormity of her workload and her complex personal circumstances. Linda had an elderly mother who required more and more care, taking up time that Linda did not have. She also felt angry that her brother who lived much closer did almost nothing and expected Linda to do it all. She told me she felt she was doing everything badly and letting everyone down. This awareness came about through listening to her non-verbal communication, and it was only when I showed that I had noticed something in her that the important details emerged.

What other types of non-verbal communication are there? What is it that we are reading or translating when we look at another person? We pick up clues from other people all the time without even being aware we are doing this. So it is important to bring what we are unaware of into our conscious thinking and responding.

✸ The next time you are travelling by train discreetly observe a person in the seats across the carriage. What is your instinctive impression about them? What are they wearing? How are they sitting? Do they look happy, sad, worried, anxious, depressed or relaxed? What body language tells you this might be the case? Do they avoid eye contact with others? Are they so busy talking about themselves (if they are with a friend or on their phone) that they do not notice other people? Your impressions may not necessarily be right, but the more often you do this the more you will hone your skills in noticing non-verbal communication.

There is no infallible technique to translating body language, but if we can take clues from non-verbal communication it offers a context or a key with which to understand what a person is really saying, thinking and feeling. A friend of mine, Harry, is a very successful car salesman. He revealed his techniques for selling expensive cars. If there were two people looking for a new car the first thing he did was work out who was the dominant partner. This would be more likely the person who would make the decision, although this was rarely the one who asked all the questions. Having done this he would then pay particular attention to their body language, focusing on their appearance, their stance, their facial expression, voice and physiological responses, and his own intuition. Beginning with appearance, he took less notice of how old or new their clothes were but guessed more from their quality. He sold upmarket Land Rovers and knew his two key customer types were farmers and more moneyed couples wanting a trendy car to do the private school run in. Appearance was more important than saving the planet. He then examined how they acted in terms of their posture, how they moved and any gestures they made. I suspect this was also a way of deciding who was dominant. When we listen to people this gives us insight into how and where they express their emotions, especially when combined with their facial expressions, such as smiling, lip movements, frowning, raised eyebrows, grimaces and laughter. Voice is also significant as the tone, pitch, volume, intensity, accent and emphases, pauses and silences are unique to every person.

Harry paid particular attention to noticeable physiological responses such as quickened breathing, red blotches appearing on the neck, blushing, or pupil dilation. He also noted mannerisms, and once told me that one of my mannerisms when I talked was twisting my wedding ring around my finger. He said that when people are moving to make a decision these physiological responses and mannerisms increase in intensity. It is at this point that he offers an extra inducement by adding a free accessory or knocking a hundred pounds off the price as a way of clinching the deal and earning his commission.

We may not be selling cars, but we still need to learn how to 'read' these messages without distorting or over-interpreting them and here we have all developed our own level of intuition. Sometimes we just know, or think we know; that is why it is important to check things out through other levels of communication that are also taking place. My one health warning is that intuition is not infallible, but is part of the range of skills we have evolved unconsciously and use a great deal more than we realize.

Having outlined some of the components of attentive listening it is also good to be aware of some of the components of *inattentive* listening, so we know what to avoid. While these are implied it is always good to spell something out so we know clearly what skills we need to develop further. In what ways can listening be inattentive? What are the signs to look out for?

1. **Interrupting.** Stopping someone while they are telling their story can be disruptive and communicates that we are not really listening to them, as we are asking a question that is more to do with satisfying our curiosity. It can also imply that the only reason we are listening is to obtain information, and once we have that we want to pull out of the conversation altogether. This is common in many work contexts that spill over into other listening arenas. People will tell us what they need to tell us, but it needs to be in their own way and in their own time. For some people this is a slow, rambling monologue that requires patience. I never said listening was easy. If you find you often interrupt people, remind yourself of what it was like when you were trying to tell someone something very important and you were interrupted. How did that make you feel?

2. **Preoccupation.** As we listen there are times when what is being said triggers a whole raft of thoughts and feelings and we drift off into our own world. When we do this we are not able to fully listen to the other person. In fact we often give physiological clues that this is happening, with less direct eye contact, shallower breathing and what could be described as a faraway look in the eyes. Sometimes we are distracted simply because we are not in a good place ourselves at that time, as after all we are only human. We are fallible, we make mistakes, we become ill, we worry, we experience loss and so there are times when we are unable to be attentive listeners. It is much better at those times to find someone who will listen to us, rather than to force ourselves to listen to others.

3. **Critical listening.** Every one of us can be critical and offer a judgement on something we have experienced. If we go to a new Balti restaurant we compare it with a previous experience that sets the standard for our culinary adventures in the curry world. Yet often such a level of critical judgement is applied to people that we become judgemental. The basis of that may be provoked by something they said that we didn't like or disagreed with. It might be our own prejudicial views that are being challenged. Or it may be we are uncovering a blind spot in our understanding of working with issues of difference and diversity. For example, I have several academic colleagues who are experts in their field, well-liked and respected, but when it comes to others talking about religion it is as if they become some other person. Religion for them is incomprehensible and as one said, 'I cannot understand how any rational intelligent person can believe in such fanciful nonsense'. This means that when it comes to religion their listening is inauthentic because they cannot hear what is being said or enter into the experience of the person who is speaking, without a critical, negative judgement making its presence felt.

4. **Rehearsed listening.** Earlier in this chapter we looked at how difficult loss and bereavement can be. If we have experienced such traumatic events we're particularly attuned to how people respond to us. If people do so with some form of rehearsed listening, it doesn't feel as if we have been listened to at all and often makes us feel worse. We can experience depression or anger at the degree of implied caring, inauthentic platitudes or inattentive listening that has been offered. I suggest that it is better to remain silent than to try to offer something that does not come from the heart. There are other forms of rehearsed listening. If we are trying to get it right as we listen to another person, thinking, 'How do I respond to this?' or 'What is the best thing to say or do at this moment?', this impedes our ability to listen.

There are many other aspects to attentive listening, and the skills required to do this will be explored later. The art of listening is always expanding and there are other areas that draw on our beliefs and values that are beyond the scope of this book (see my previous book *Counselling Skills for Church and Faith Community Workers* for a more detailed look at this). These other dimensions of listening include recognizing a spiritual dimension, observing the influence of our gender, embodiment and sexuality, and locating social, political and cultural contexts. So listening is much more complicated and challenging than it might at first assumed to be. The stereotype of listening, 'More tea, vicar?', could not be further from the truth. The ability to hear what people are actually saying and to acknowledge the depth of their feelings produces a rich appreciation of the value and complexity of the individual to whom we are listening. In being listened to attentively by us they may also begin to discover these aspects of themselves in new ways.

The next step is to put these attentive listening skills in the wider context of establishing a relationship, and this is the focus of the next chapter.

9. Establishing a relationship

I don't want to frighten you again, and I know I asked you to think about your death in the previous chapter, but now I want you to think back to your adolescence. I'm sorry if this wrecks years of therapy, but imagine the boy or girl you first fell in love with (not counting the crush you might have had on your teacher). Some of you (and me) are blushing or feeling embarrassed already. Just try to recall how long it took you to build up the courage to speak to them, or even get them to acknowledge you existed at all. The idea of a real flesh-and-blood relationship was a fantasy that filled your dreams, day and night. Now fast forward your memories to your first actual relationship. What was it like? How agonizing was that initial decision to ask them out and the utter shock and amazement when they agreed? How vital was it that they didn't reject you, turning your dreams to nightmares? How awful was it when it all came crashing down, and all life seemed to end, or so we felt at the time?

Clearly relationships are an essential part of being human. In fact many theologians and pioneering psychoanalytic thinkers believe that to be human is to be in relationship – we are born relationship-seeking. Just as a newborn baby searches for a breast when hungry, there is a psychological equivalent of searching for people and the relationships they bring. Put simply, we need other people and engaging in relationships with them is what makes us human. It's why we so long for relationships and find loneliness or isolation so difficult to bear. This is beautifully captured in some words from Mother Theresa of Calcutta: 'The greatest disease in the West today is not TB or leprosy; it is being unwanted, unloved, and uncared for. We can cure physical diseases with medicine, but the only cure for loneliness, despair and hopelessness is love. There are many in the world who are dying for a piece of bread but there are many more dying for a little love.'

People seek and are hungry for relationships, but as we already know from adolescence, relationships do not come with guarantees and are fraught with difficulties. Think for a moment about the friends we have fallen out with over the years. Sometimes responsibility for what went wrong lies with us. Maybe we simply grew out of the relationship. Going away to university while friends stay at home, and leaving friends from university to start a career in another part of the country are just some of the hurdles that friendships stumble over. Our life experience gives us a fresh or different perspective, which enables us to see ourselves and other people in a new light. So every new relationship brings with it the hope of new opportunity as well as ghosts of past relationships. But why is this significant for our learning to use counselling skills?

Every relationship requires a level of mutual respect, being able to trust the other person and an ability to communicate and to be on the same wavelength. Sometimes this comes through slowly building trust, step by step. At other times it blossoms out of a shared set of experiences. Occasionally it is instant and we 'hit it off' immediately for reasons we can or cannot fathom. Remember Sue from the introduction to part two? She and Becky, the only two six-foot-tall girls in the school, became instant friends. United by their height they also found a sense of each other that became important to them. Yet other friends appear to have nothing in common but somehow 'met'. These are common features of the many different kinds of relationships that exist. I have a good working relationship with Penny, my administrator. I expect her to fulfil a role and have found that if you let people get on and use their range of skills rather than micromanage every task and decision it leads to a much better and more productive working relationship. Would I offer Penny counselling if she experienced difficulties? No, because it would break the boundary of our working relationship. However, I would listen and support, helping her to discover what she needed for herself. So a working or professional relationship does not preclude the use of counselling and attentive listening skills.

If you have been listening to the other person in the way we have just outlined, you have already laid a substantial foundation for establishing a relationship. The person we are listening to will feel they have been heard as a person in and through our presence and may choose to take that further. Notice it really needs to be their choice. Sometimes people can be taken by surprise at being listened to and as a consequence reveal far more than they later feel comfortable with. They may want to put some distance between us and them and take things more slowly. Just because we make a profound connection with someone does not mean it will be like this every time. All relationships have boundaries in order for us to know how they work and who fits where.

The use of counselling skills offers the opportunity to enhance a relationship, but these skills must be used with caution. Remember, it is far easier to take something apart than it is to put it together again. People are not like IKEA furniture. Despite the instructions that come with flat-pack furniture you need to build yourself, I always get one bit wrong, but at least with furniture you can just undo various screws and bolts and redo them in the right order. You can't do that with people. Using attentive listening skills and building a relationship with someone allows us to support them so that they can get the help they need, which may be a formal counselling relationship with a qualified and professionally accredited counsellor.

Yet there is also a context to forming a listening relationship. The location where we listen to people is also significant. While on journeys, holidays, weekend events, training conferences and other social events we can form brief relationships with people, but this context means that it is unlikely this will lead to an ongoing relationship. Yet even here there is always the potential for the unexpected. When our children were little we went on holiday to a family hotel in Cornwall, which after our previous very wet summer holidays had the added attraction of an indoor swimming pool. We met another family with children the same age and we subsequently spent a lot of time together either around the pool or in the hotel's children's playground and gardens. Later in the week the mother, Rachel, said that she found it difficult to talk to me because I seemed to be able to see inside her head – I had simply been using my normal attentive listening skills. She went on to say that she wanted both to talk to me and not to talk to me. At the end of the week during a long sunny afternoon, while our partners were looking after the children, she took the courage to tell me about aspects of her life. This included disclosing that she had been sexually abused by her father, a fact she had never disclosed to anyone other than her partner. She said it felt such a relief to tell someone who would understand and most importantly someone she was not likely to see again. So Rachel is out there somewhere and I have no idea of how her life unfolded, but what I do know is that attentive listening made a difference for her at that time. She took a risk and felt a great sense of relief as her shame was heard by another who didn't judge or condemn.

Wherever we find ourselves and meet other people we can still enhance their (and our) experience through good attentive listening. There are a number of simple skills that aid this and have been summed up in the acronym SOLER, developed by Gerard Egan in his book *The Skilled Helper*. Simply being with another person, or 'attending' as Egan describes it, gives the other person the cues that we are interested in listening to them.

SOLER sometimes adapted to become SOLAR (where the A stands for 'appropriate').

Squarely. Sit facing the person squarely within a comfortable distance so as to be able to hear what they say. This reveals we are interested in the person, implying, 'I am available to you'. Don't take this too literally as you can still talk attentively to somebody in the car, plane or train, even though this puts you side by side. Yet talking to somebody who is sitting behind a desk feels very different, which may create some form of psychological barrier between you.

Open. Adopt an open posture. Have you ever noticed that if you are speaking to someone you don't really want to your body language becomes closed, through folding arms or crossing legs? Often we turn away from the person, not quite turning our back on them, but indicating that we don't really want to be there. By contrast, a relaxed, open posture gives a sign that we are open to the person and to what he or she has to say. We are open literally and metaphorically. Having adopted this open posture it is also important to maintain it so as not to give confusing signals to the person, making them think we are shutting down or turning away because of something they have said.

Lean. The British violin player Nigel Kennedy said recently that he wants to play music that people lean into, that moves them to be engaged, as if they are sitting on the edge of their seats. Leaning toward the client (when appropriate) can show your involvement and interest as if you want to know more and to know it now, in this moment. Leaning back from someone you are listening to may convey the opposite message, as if you are pulling back from what they have said or are no longer interested. We also need to be aware of our personal style. Leaning back can also show we are relaxed and enjoying the presence of the other person, so this needs to be understood in context (see below).

Eye. Maintaining good or appropriate eye contact with a person communicates interest, concern, or warmth. While such eye contact could be too challenging or disrespectful in some cultural contexts, it is something we normally expect on an unconscious level. We see it as a sign that someone is interested in who we are and what we're saying. In the same way, if someone we are talking to continually looks away we assume we are uninteresting, boring or that they are uncomfortable with what we are saying.

Relaxed. Communication is always more effective when we are relaxed or natural with the other person. The ability to be relaxed means you show that you are comfortable, and this is often expressed through your body. This allows people to feel at ease. It is always helpful not to fidget nervously as the other person may begin to wonder if it's them that is making you nervous.

When you first try these skills, often described as micro skills, they can feel artificial – as if you are engineering a particular kind of conversation. Don't worry, soon they will become second nature to you, especially when you realize that you've probably been using them all along in any good listening you have automatically done. Attentive listening forms the foundations of relationships when we demonstrate that we are present for the other person. Our sense of presence to the other person has been communicated by the eye contact we have established and maintained, an open body stance that shows we are relaxed in their presence but engaged and interested in what they have to say, and a volume and tone of voice that matches the other person's and fits the subject being talked about, especially when allied to an appropriate warmth that reveals an empathic understanding. How we take this relationship forward requires another set of skills – such as developing empathy and the use and place of silence – which we shall examine in a later chapter. But first it is vital that we examine the subject of confidentiality, as this provides another way in which the person feels safe in our presence and therefore able to reveal more of who they truly are and want to be.

10. Feeling safe and confidentiality

When we feel safe we can relax, sensing that we are in a place or with people that offer presence, support and trust. The best illustration of that is to see a baby asleep while being held in its mother's, father's or grandparents' arms. The big wide world and whatever it brings is held back while the bliss of sleep engulfs this small, vulnerable infant. As children and adults, if we do not feel safe we feel wary or anxious. We feel on edge, ready to run at any moment. All attentive listening requires the person to feel safe and one vital way to do this is through offering confidentiality.

Confidentiality forms the heart of all counselling and therapeutic relationships and, I suggest, all helping relationships using counselling or attentive listening skills. It is a sign of respect for the person we are listening to as well as a vital way of establishing trust in any relationship. In BACP's *Ethical Framework for Good Practice in Counselling and Psychotherapy* (2013) confidentiality is described as a fundamental concept that forms the core of the way in which counselling and counselling skill best values all people. Confidentiality is often assumed but should never be taken for granted.

Kathy began to tell me about her son in a lunchtime conversation. This is not a counselling relationship but one where I offer support to her from time to time just by listening. Kathy shared more detail than she had in the past and at one point I said, 'Kathy, thank you for telling me this. Just so you are sure, I consider that what you are telling me is confidential, and it's not something I talk about with others.' Kathy replied 'I sort of expected that, but it is good to hear.'

There are many relationships that because of their nature imply confidentiality, such as doctor/nurse-patient, therapist-client, or solicitor-client. This is less clear when we are using counselling skills in an informal context. It's therefore always helpful to clarify this, as shown above. But as good as confidentiality is as an ethical principle and counselling practice, we should never fall into the trap of guaranteeing absolute confidentiality. This is for the simple reason that we can never deliver on this promise and for other reasons we shall explore shortly. While a Roman Catholic priest accepts the absolute duty of never disclosing anything that they learn during the sacrament of confession even on pain of their death or the deaths of others, this is not a legal protection in English or Scottish courts.

Imagine for a moment how shaming and damaging it would be if after you had revealed your innermost fear to somebody you trusted, you discovered that they had posted details on their Facebook page or Twitter feed: 'Saw a really troubled person today, abused from the age of three, no wonder they are self-harming and suicidal. Don't see much hope.' Even if you were not named, the sense of betrayal would be enormous because you believed what you had said would be held in confidence. Confidentiality is central.

Most people assume that if they reveal something personal about themselves then this is viewed as confidential. Yet if it is so important, why does confidentiality get broken? Here is a list of the common reasons:

1. **Unintentionally.** Sometimes we pass information on without thinking, especially if holding information in a confidential manner is something we are not used to. If this does happen it is always best to tell the person concerned what has been said and take any fallout from this honest mistake. This communicates that we respect them and understand that we have acted in an unhelpful way.

2. **Pressure.** We can be put under pressure by someone who knows we have access to information that they want and who employs all means to

obtain this from us. This is more likely in a work context rather than in a helping role in which we have used our counselling skills. This happened to me, and under pressure I revealed the name of a person after agreeing our conversations would be confidential. On later reflection I realized I had done the wrong thing and apologized to the person concerned. This helped repair a relationship that had become fractured. I was less forgiving of my senior colleague who had put me in such a difficult position and used their power in a way I felt was inappropriate and exploitative.

3. **Burden.** The burden of information shared is sometimes just too great for the person listening to bear. Thinking about Rachel mentioned in the previous chapter I suspect she trusted me because I was a therapist and not just an attentive listener. For some people what she shared could have been too difficult (especially if it had touched on issues of their own that were similar) and led them to talk to another person, such as a partner. Counsellors are better equipped in this context as they have a clinical supervisor for their therapeutic work. The idea that a counsellor has supervision is included in any discussion of confidentiality with clients at the start of the counselling relationship. I was video recording my use of a new therapeutic technique (dynamic interpersonal therapy) and the client asked who would see the video. I mentioned it would be seen by me, my clinical supervisor and in case of technical difficulties, by a video technician in transferring the material to disc. They replied this was fine as their concern was that it would be used in some form of teaching.

4. **Gossip.** Think for a moment of the one person among your friends and acquaintances you would least like to share any personal or confidential information with. Why? Because you know that if you did your 'secret' would have been passed on to others. Before we get too superior and think that is something we could never do, remember we all like having knowledge and passing it on. We like being on the inside, having special or unique knowledge. It is just that for some this spills over into gossip.

5. **Exploitation.** Some information can be exploited commercially, even if this is unethical and in most cases, illegal. There have been a number of high-profile court cases where individuals, having gained confidential information, have sold this to newspapers and private information has

been published. If this were to occur, chapter 6 outlines what initial steps you could take.

6. **Legal constraints.** There are legal requirements that mean if certain information is shared, even in a casual conversation as we use listening skills, it has to be reported. This applies to all people, not just counsellors. Statutory law overturns the legal right to confidentiality. These laws primarily relate to terrorism, having caused serious harm or the intention to do so, serious crime including money laundering and the abuse or risk of abuse to children. While you are required to report such concerns to the appropriate authorities it is also possible to get the person we are listening to informally, or the client we are seeing as a counsellor, to do this themselves. However the responsibility cannot simply be handed back to the person. If they do not self-report any listener or counsellor is required to take action.

7. **Potential harm to self.** This is a more complex grey area that tries to take into account a person's right to decide for themself (the ethical principle of autonomy we discussed earlier). Some areas of confidentiality need to be balanced with a clinical judgement. Suicide in particular is always a difficult subject. In counselling clients may talk about suicide and the counsellor will need to make a judgement as to the level of risk involved. The best course of action is always to help a client to come to their own decision so that the issue of a breach of confidentiality doesn't come into question.

8. **Specific contexts involving children.** Counselling being made available in school contexts has been a growing trend that I think will reap long-term benefits both for individuals and society at large. It's not without complications, however, especially in this area of confidentiality. Each school, local authority and the police has guidelines for best practice in balancing the needs and rights of the child, as well as their capacity to decide independently of a parent, parents or carers. This is within the context of formal counselling; however with children information is often shared early on in informal conversations with people who will listen.

I used to be a volunteer helper in a specialist twin health centre in Birmingham. I offered my therapeutic expertise to any parent or parents in consultation with the paediatrician when required. In the meantime I used to be available to play imaginatively with any of the twins, triplets or other multiples. I was playing cooking with five-year-old Sarah, twin sister of Simon, who said, 'I like you, you are a friendly man.' After we cooked pretend tea Sarah added, 'The man next door, he smells but he gives me sweets. I like sweets.' After a pause, 'I don't like things he does.' If I did not act on this information I could be putting Sarah and Simon at some form of risk yet it came about because of attentive listening and playing, not counselling.

As you have been reading your way through this book I have introduced a large number of clinical snapshots of my experiences of using attentive listening and counselling skills. For reasons of confidentiality, while all these examples are rooted in real-life experiences, they have been disguised so that no actual person in a clinical case is recognizable. I have variously changed gender, age, location, context and some are composite characters combining elements from a number of different clients. I did once have a client who was convinced she was one of my clients in a previous book, although this gave us plenty to work on in therapy. I also had one client who volunteered to be in any future book as long as she could choose her name. Coming back to thinking about developing our attentive listening and counselling skills, the next chapter reveals other skills we can develop to enhance our abilities.

So having taken a detour into the serious end of the confidentiality spectrum it is important to focus back on where we started. This is that confidentiality reflects the foundation of all trusting relationships, which respect the person and all they share. It should be seen as a hallmark of a depth of engagement rather than as an ethical challenge or problem to be solved.

11. Using questions, exploring, clarifying, summarizing and paraphrasing

Now you have learnt to listen attentively, have established a relationship and have become aware of the person's context through reading their body language and making a safe space through awareness of confidentiality – what happens next? Where do we go from here?

Using Questions

When people tell us stories they miss bits out, jump around in time, move from the past into the present, introduce a whole cast of characters, mention assorted family members, lose themselves in feelings or reflections and often speak in incomplete sentences. We use talking as a way of untangling this confusion. We talk it out to clarify and express existing feelings, as well as discovering new feelings that can take us by surprise. If you have ever conducted an interview and tried to make sense of the jumble of words afterwards you will know exactly what I mean. There is a reason why some people are journalists; they are able to craft a story out of that muddle. Yet using questions at the right time and in the right way can help the person we are listening to tell their story in greater depth and in new ways. Asking open-ended questions, questions that require more than a simple 'yes' or 'no' answer, opens out the conversation. For example, one response could be, 'That sounds really interesting, tell me more about …' or, 'When that happened I wonder what you felt …' Asking a question is very different from making a statement that closes down the opportunity for the person to say more. While making statements can be helpful in the right place, as we shall see a little later, they can often seem like an implied judgement. If someone said to me, 'Well that's all in the past, we don't need to dwell on that anymore' I would feel they don't really want to listen to me, or worse, that they don't believe me. As a therapist I have listened to a wide range of clients, many of whom have some form of sexual abuse in their background. Interestingly this is not always what they are seeking counselling for. Yet all of them have wanted to be believed and many recall that the first time they told another person they were shunned, ignored, thrown out of the family for telling 'horrible lies' or simply told to 'shut up'. This leads to even greater self-condemnation and becoming fearful of saying such a thing ever again. It can restrict them from saying more as they never want another rejection that touches the very core of their being.

By contrast, open-ended questions feel less threatening or intrusive. They encourage or invite more detail or description and let a narrative unfold. When I did my initial counselling skills training we did an exercise where one person played the role of a client telling about an emotional event in their life. Another played the role of a counsellor helping the person make sense of what they were talking about. A third person acted as an observer noting the body language of the 'client' and the counselling skills of the 'counsellor' including the types of questions they used. I was playing the role of the counsellor and in the limited time available wanted to get as much information as possible. When it came to the feedback from the observer after the exercise had finished, they said that I had bombarded the client with a lot of closed questions. A closed question is one where there are 'yes' or 'no' answers such as 'Did you go to the home?' or 'Is that what you said?' The client said they had felt 'grilled', as if it had been a police interrogation. It was an early and important lesson for me – I had let my anxiety to be seen to be doing something overrule my normal listening skills. I might also have fallen into the trap of wanting to do something and so I asked questions because I didn't know what else to do. Questions should be used sparingly as a way of moving the story on or helping it reach a new depth. It is helpful to avoid asking one question after another without letting the person have time to fill the space between if they want.

At this point it is important to point out that asking the question 'Why?' is rarely helpful. If the person we are listening to knew the answer they would probably not be talking to us. It also assumes there is a rational answer to the question, 'Why?'

I once spent some time listening to Liz, who became paralyzed from the waist down in her early twenties due to the sudden onset of multiple sclerosis. At that time I had not done any counselling or listening skills training. I felt out of my depth and because of that stayed quiet and listened. In hindsight it was by far the best thing I could have done. She said, 'People often ask me the question "why?" but in reality the question is "why not?" Nobody is immune from illness, suffering, and tragedy, so why should I be any different? Don't get me wrong, I am not some kind of masochist and of course there are days when I wish it had not happened, but this is my life and I can either choose to live it as best I can or descend into the bitterness that I see in others in my situation. I am not judging them as I know how hard it is, but I am choosing what's best for me.'

Encouraging exploration and seeking clarification

These are good reasons for asking questions in a way that is tentative, exploratory and non-confrontational. In ordinary conversation people will hear what we say and express their feelings, such as, 'I can't believe you said that …' or 'You said *what*?' These are statements and do not invite further exploration. Instead, an explorative response could be, 'That provoked a strong reaction; I wonder what else was going on?' There are times when we can use statements, questions, requests such as 'Tell me more …', 'I was thinking …', 'When you said that I felt…', or 'I guess … but what was happening for you?' We can also use single words or phrases such as 'Yes', 'Hmm' or even a sigh that indicates you are still listening and engaged but don't want to interrupt. This can also be accompanied by non-verbal prompts through eye contact, a smile (in the right place of course), or an open body position, leaning forwards and not crossing our arms or legs in a way that looks defensive. These are aspects of attentive listening which enable people to explore their important issues or discover their unexpressed feelings more fully.

✳   The next time you are listening to someone, such as a partner, friend or colleague, try the following. Firstly, say as little as possible, and when you do, stick with the information the person has given you and use the following phrase: 'That sounds really helpful' (assuming it was of course). Pause and don't give in to the temptation to say more. Let it settle and wait. This opens up a space for your friend to say more if they want; it is an invitation to explore further. Secondly, you can move this conversation further forward by clarifying an issue without letting this dominate or divert the main focus of the person, taking the attention away from their conversation. You could try: 'When you said that it felt like there were some other things that had not yet been said …' These have the effect of keeping the focus on the person but moving their story forward, giving the opportunity for new layers of the story, often related to feelings, to emerge.

Summarizing and Paraphrasing

These are two other skills that are often used in attentive listening. As we have already seen, when people tell stories they tend not to do so in a coherent fashion and part of the point of listening is to help piece together the whole picture. At the other end of the spectrum, sometimes because of the person's circumstances and the events surrounding them, they may have had to tell their story again and again. One way of dealing with this is to develop an edited version of the story covering the bare facts but that doesn't get caught up in the painful feelings that are often associated.

Colin was injured in a car crash on a motorway that left him with a head injury and several broken limbs. His car had been side-swiped by a lorry, sending him into the barriers on the central reservation, and the emergency services had to cut him out of the wreckage. He was treated quickly and made good progress with a broken arm and leg, but could not recall the accident. He was interviewed by the police as they were considering charging the lorry driver for driving while being on his mobile phone. Colin could still not remember and felt increasingly depressed. His head injury took much longer to heal and he spent months in a head injury unit to enable him to regain normal functioning. Different professionals asked Colin about the accident so many times that he developed a rehearsed narrative. Due to his depression, a year after the accident Colin came for counselling. As I listened to his story I offered back to him a summary of what he had said, not in his exact words but in a paraphrase – a condensed version of what he said but in a way that also helped him see that he had been listened to, so there was room for new insights to emerge.

Colin: 'I still can't remember. It sort of came out of nowhere and then it all goes dark and the next thing I know there is this grinding noise and I see sparks. I don't know where I am, I feel trapped and I started to panic but realized there was someone next to me saying it was OK, that I had been in an accident and that they needed to cut open the car. I know it is bizarre but my first thoughts were "My mum is going to kill me." Her car was her pride and joy and they had just cut the roof off. The next thing I really remember is lying in the ambulance, my head spinning around, feeling sick but with a paramedic talking to me. No idea what he said …?'

Me: 'You've told me what you can remember from your accident, which sounds quite terrifying but at crucial times there were people there making you feel it was OK.'

While Colin's case is more complicated, summarizing and paraphrasing can be as simple as saying, 'You must have felt really devastated when that happened.' This helps the people we listen to more clearly identify experiences and feelings that give a richer, broader and deeper picture to their story. Colin's early concern was less for his own health, as his 'devastation' was around what his mum was going to feel with her car missing a roof. This response from the listener filled in a missing piece of the picture as everyone was focusing on Colin.

These active steps in attentive listening are helpful especially if the person is a little reluctant to tell their story. Because they have previously experienced inattentive listening many people don't just leap in, but will wait to see how we respond. Using open questions, exploring comments and clarifying statements, alongside summarizing and paraphrasing help keep the focus on the person and their story, but also helps them to move forward from being stuck in a narrative roundabout. These skills enable them to discover a range of thoughts and feelings that were just waiting to be articulated. Yet it is also very important to note how exhausting this whole process can be. Listening and being with people, attending to their pain, complexities, traumas, losses and confusion can leave us drained. It can also touch on areas of our own life and affect our own thoughts and feelings. So it is vital that all people, whether they are using counselling skills or offering counselling, have the capacity to look after themselves and find suitable support and supervision.

The next chapter focuses on two skills that relate to not just what we do, but how we are with the person when we offer affirmation and demonstrate empathy.

12. Affirmation, empathy, respect and non-judgement

What exactly is affirmation? Let me use a personal example. I, like many people, have a love-hate affair with physical fitness and going to the gym. My fantasy is that by taking out a gym membership I will magically get fit. The reality is that not only do I need to attend but I need expert advice about what to do and how to best help my arthritic knees. After I booked a session with Louise, a physiotherapist and personal trainer, she designed a 48-minute programme, working on the principle that a shorter programme is more likely to be completed. As she took me through these various exercises she made encouraging comments like, 'you're doing really well' or, 'that's good, keep it up, just a few more stretches' and so on. I felt pleased and encouraged. I felt that she was noticing that I was making an effort to engage in this process. It also alerted me to the fact that in some part of my mind there was a nagging, critical voice that I had expected to say 'you're not fit enough' or 'you are not trying'.

How vitally important is it that we all experience affirmation, and what exactly is it? Affirmation is recognition by another person of who and what we are. It is being seen as a person in a whole sense and it's increasingly necessary today as it has so often been missing from people's early experiences, leaving them feeling they are never good enough. It is such a straightforward step, but offering affirmation to someone recognizes that they are a person with thoughts and feelings that are valid and meaningful.

Try to recall the last time you experienced affirmation. What did that feel like? Can you recall how old (or young) you were when you were experiencing this? Who offered this to you and why?

As we have seen we all need affirmation. This is especially the case when someone has shared personal or sensitive information with us. Remember Rachel who I met on holiday, described in chapter 9? Her disclosure that she had been sexually abused required acceptance and affirmation in recognition of the risk she had taken and the trust she had given to me. It felt a real privilege to listen to her story, painful as it was. My response to Rachel was affirming, and the phrase I used was along the lines of, 'Thank you for sharing that, it must have taken real courage.' As with all responses we always need to be alert to the danger of being formulaic, or saying the right words but without the required feeling. So affirmation is more than just encouraging words. It is recognition of the other person, including their faults and failings, hopes and dreams, potentials and futures. It is a way of relating to someone that encourages the person they are deep down, not simply the task or role they perform. What is also so important about affirmation is that it links with empathy.

Empathy is the ability to hear, see, think and feel the world through the experience of the other person. It is the willingness to try to make sense of what you hear. Harper Lee in the novel *To Kill a Mockingbird* writes, 'You never really know a man until you understand things from his point of view, until you climb into his skin and walk around in it.' Empathy is the ability to 'walk in another's shoes', without thinking that our experience will be the same as theirs. Empathy attempts to understand the other person we are listening to on their own terms and also requires that we communicate our understanding to them. Note I say 'attempt', because there are some stories we will be told that we cannot fully enter into because we have not had that experience. This does not disqualify us from helping, but attentive listening comes into play here to show that we are listening in depth and engaged with the person, believing their story, not offering slick answers or solutions to make the problem go away because it is too painful for us to hear.

Empathy requires checking out that what we are saying relates to their experience and captures how they think and feel.

✳   Mike said, 'I'm really worried about failing my viva (a verbal examination used for research degrees). I've written my thesis and I am pretty confident it is OK, but I am scared that when I get into that room I will go blank and just stand there looking like an idiot, not knowing anything. I am never good under pressure and the last time I had an interview I forgot everything I was going to say. I felt so stupid.'

Which of the following responses best demonstrates the use of empathic listening skills?

1. 'You'll be fine. There's no need to worry. I am sure the last time was just a blip.'
2. 'I know what you mean. I used to be like that but I found if I concentrated on four key ideas I fixed in my mind beforehand it was OK.'
3. 'You're clearly feeling anxious about your viva, and worried that you'll go blank like you did once before. Tell me what it felt like the last time?'

The first response attempts to be reassuring but feels dismissive as it does not touch on the person's feelings of failure from before. These get glossed over. The second response focuses on the experience of the person listening but reveals they have not really listened to the emotional context that the student has clearly communicated. The third response is empathic as the listener has briefly summed up the issue, identified the underlying feelings of anxiety, communicated the deep-seated fear of being stupid (broadening this out to be inclusive), and then used an exploratory question or prompt to allow the person to continue their story.

The experience of having someone listen in an empathic way can touch us at a deep level and have a profound effect on us, even if it is only a very brief exchange. It is a skill that all of us can develop and use that really helps other people. We saw earlier that it is vital for human development that we develop a sense of being an 'I'; a person with identity and agency. But it is just as important that we develop a sense of the 'other' and what it is like to be another person. It shows us the world in new ways.

In counselling training empathy is seen as a basic and essential skill. It's developed into advanced empathy by taking a step further and linking the spoken narrative (i.e. what has been said) with the unspoken narrative. Often people will hint at something just below the surface that attentive listening picks up on, and which can be further revealed through an empathic response. Such skills usually require further and specialist training. As we get to know people through listening to their stories and as they reveal depths about themselves we use both empathy and respect. We have already touched on the former but we shall now examine the latter.

Respect

There are two kinds of respect. The first is a recognition we give to people who have achieved something incredible, or reached a level we aspire to. We know how much work is involved in getting to this standard. Last summer I went climbing in the Cullin mountain range on the Isle of Skye. These are rightly regarded as the best and most challenging mountains in the UK. We hired a local mountain guide, Graham, who had vast experience, and at each stage of the day my respect for him grew as I saw his expertise at work. I noted not just how he ensured people's safety but how he engaged each person differently to meet their particular needs, and encouraged us to achieve our physical potential and reach the summits. Very sadly Graham was killed in a climbing accident at the end of last year and will be missed by many.

Yet there is a second kind of respect that grows out of not what a person has done, but your sense of what they will do. Given the awful events some people have been through there is a respect that they have survived at all. This grows into an even greater respect that in trusting themselves, helped by your attentive listening, they will be able to fulfil more of their potential. Your respect for them, conveyed through the way you listen and how you respond empathically, enables new opportunities that their past could potentially have robbed them of. This kind of respect is simply valuing the person you see before you, and is sensed by the other person.

Non-judgement

Respect for the person and what they say, think, and feel is a building block for an empathic response, especially when it is allied to acceptance and a non-judgemental approach. We make judgements all the time, consciously and unconsciously. We judge whether it is better for us to eat a slice of cheesecake or an apple. We judge how much time it takes to drive to a meeting. We judge whether a colleague's work reaches the required standard. We judge whether the current government is doing a good job on the NHS. Most of these have a rational basis and can be debated. But we can also make judgements about people based on certain stereotypes, viewing them as a category rather than an individual. At its worst it can be racist, sexist and homophobic, but even in milder cases many of us have preconceived ideas about certain 'types' of people.

One of the challenges we all face is to identify how we respond to people who are different from us, who we don't fully understand, and who we might feel superior to because we are 'not like them' or they are 'not like us'. If not checked it can lead to sweeping and damaging generalizations. At an individual level we all know what it is like to have been discriminated against and judged negatively. It leaves us shocked, angry and with overwhelming feelings of being powerless. Self-blame or self-loathing often occurs in these instances; we turn anger in on ourselves as it is too dangerous to express it in other ways.

A very powerful impact can be made on another person and their story by us simply hearing, believing, accepting and not judging. It allows them to feel it is OK to be human. This was an idea first developed by Carl Rogers as another one of the core conditions that enables a person to discover who and what they are. 'Unconditional positive regard', also called non-judgemental warmth or acceptance, can repair so many of the critical judgements someone has experienced throughout their life, that have left them feeling a failure or not good enough.

✳ Make a list of the critical, negative judgements that have been made about you in the last three months. Some of these comments will have been communicated directly (sometimes under the apparently helpful guise of constructive criticism), but a great deal of communication happens indirectly, though inference, a hint, a look, a body stance of turning away, a sigh, a tone of voice or an unwillingness to look you in the eye. What effect do these judgements have on you? How do they affect your confidence or your sense of self? Now try to think of the critical, negative judgements you may have levelled at other people. How could you have more helpfully responded?

♀ When I was starting a new career in a new part of the country, a friend of a friend offered to assist me. This was a huge help. In part it was practical help; he offered me somewhere to stay while I searched for a flat to rent, and drove me around to look at them. But in one particularly grim flat on the last day of my searching he said, 'I am sure there is a better place for you than this'. This gave me the courage to act on my feelings rather than accept something out of a panic I wouldn't find anywhere. He was intuitively using the skills of affirmation, empathy, respect and acceptance. I felt relaxed, welcomed and allowed to find my own opinions without being judged.

Before we draw together the qualities and skills of attentive listening there are three other areas I wanted us to explore as these can have a significant impact on how we are with other people.

13. Finding focus and identifying steps forward

At a recent research conference the Friday night was given over to a ceilidh, which is a Gaelic word meaning an informal gathering, involving story-telling, singing or dancing. The ceilidhs I have attended always involve dancing, and a 'caller' explains the steps everyone makes. One dance involved twirling a colleague, Kate, around almost off her feet down the line of other dancers. The next day her friend said to me that the best bit of the evening had been seeing Kate's face caught between sheer enjoyment and utter terror as she had never done such a dance before. Figuring out a path through counselling conversations is a little bit like trying to find a pattern of steps for a dance for the first time: it leaves us feeling cumbersome and as if we're always tripping over ourselves. But a few 'dances' later we discover we have 'found our feet' and relax into the fun and enjoyment of other people.

Attentive listening offers the opportunity to help someone else find a focus. People talk because they are not sure what it is that is bothering them. They are confused by feelings that arrive unexpectedly or seem out of proportion to the event that triggered them. It can feel like so many things are going on at the same time that we can't see the wood for the trees. Some forms of counselling place great importance on finding this focus and identifying a problem to work on and a goal to achieve. Gerard Egan's influential book *The Skilled Helper* is subtitled 'A problem-management approach to helping' and describes three stages: helping clients identify and clarify problem situations; helping clients create a better future; and helping clients implement their goals. Attentive listening doesn't offer such a detailed way of working, but it does offer the ability to help someone identify what it is they are struggling with – which may not be immediately obvious. With the right support through attentive listening people can discover their own wisdom and insights into themselves, as each person is the best expert on their own lives; it is just that sometimes they need someone to help them understand this and put it into practice.

The other way in which finding a focus is like learning a dance is that not all the steps are in the same order, as there is a dynamic movement backwards and forwards between the person talking and the person listening. Any conversation can finish at any step and the person will have had a 'good enough' experience. People need to be allowed to say as much, or as little, as they want. It can be tantalizing being left on the cliff edge of a story wanting to know the outcome, yet that is more about satisfying our own curiosity. It may also mean they can come back at a later stage to take their initial conversation further and we might then find out the end of the story, or more likely be introduced to another chapter.

Let's sum up the three steps of the attentive listening process that we've been examining throughout this book:

Step 1

Person: Begins to say something about themselves and starts to tell their story, albeit tentatively, giving signs that they want you to listen.

Listener: Notices that the other person has moved from general social conversation and is starting to talk about themselves in a more personal way. Starts attentive listening, taking notice of the other person's body language. Begins to offer a matching response to the person through using relevant SOLAR skills.

Step 2

Person: Feels they are being heard and so offers more detail, adding depth and complexity. They can also start telling a narrative that is important to them, which they want to be heard by you.

Listener: Using summarizing and paraphrasing, gives implicit permission for the person to go further and explore even if only their confusion or lack of focus.

Person: Offers feelings, emotions and thoughts that are less refined or processed, trusting the listener to handle these or hold them until they make a bit more sense. Adds new material to their narrative as they feel they are not only being heard but understood.

Step 3

Listener: Responds by offering affirmation, empathy and respect. This is accompanied by an accepting and non-judgemental stance which often has a huge impact on the other person.

Person: Relaxes and feels safe, believed, relieved and able to focus on an area, issue or feeling that can be explored in the limited time available.

These three steps lead to a reflection on the focus or direction that can help the person being listened to. You need to bear in mind that this is not a counselling session with boundaries, which can last for nearly an hour. Some conversations will happen once and never be repeated because of the circumstances. I have had several conversations on transatlantic plane journeys where I have learnt a great deal about the other person and offered back attentive listening and focus in return. As Joel (on his way to New York) said, following our conversation about him meeting his girlfriend again after a year in Europe and having to make his mind up about making a commitment to her, 'That's amazing, how did you do that? I didn't realize I had all these feelings hidden away.' Through attentive listening I had enabled Joel to identify his feelings about his girlfriend, including the realization that by going to Europe he had, in part, been running away from making a commitment to her. Without intending to set any goal for our conversation (that took place over three periods between watching the latest films), Joel organically came to find his own focus and identified the steps he wanted to take forward in his forthcoming conversation with his girlfriend.

The diagram below outlines these three steps in another way:

Person	Dynamic flow	Listener
Shares a personal story, offering cues		Listens – using attentive listening skills. Picks up cues
Experiences being listened to and adds more detail		Offers summarizing, paraphrasing and exploring
Feels able to reveal confusion, conflict and feelings		Offers affirmation, empathy, respect, and does not judge
Experiences a 'safe' space and the opportunity to say more		Respectful engagement leads to clearer focus 'Let me tell you what I have heard'
Impact: Catharsis 'I am believed' Insight 'I can see things differently' Agency 'I want to focus on …'		Offers presence that is a containing of thoughts and feelings with a boundaried, respectful attentiveness

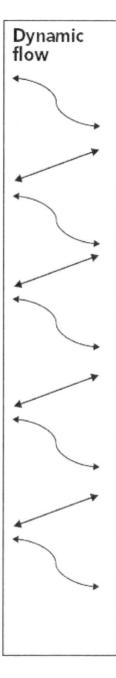

14. Exploring silence, the unconscious, and creating a sense of presence

I have various friends who do triathlons, run marathons, get involved in charity cycle events, and canoe down river gorges, all of which I understand. Yet there are others who do extreme endurance events, pushing their bodies to the absolute limit. I find myself asking the question 'Why'?

One answer is that we define ourselves through the physical and mental tests we can endure. Yet I realized that while my body could never take on such extreme challenges, as a therapist there are times when my psyche is pushed to extreme limits through the shared pain I experience in the lives of many of my clients. So when life gets unbearably tough or fractured into many pieces, what is it that people need? What is it that helps – or to be more personal, what would really help you? This could be a long list but includes: to be noticed, to be heard and to be loved. We are hungry for all of these, and their absence shapes our distinctive way of being and relating. How do we experience this when outside of a contained, boundary-filled counselling or therapeutic context?

People have so many untold stories they long for someone to listen to. Once that basic trust has been established I am constantly amazed at just what people will share, revealing narratives filled with trauma, pain and tragedy. Yet despite this there is also the presence of courage, resilience and hope.

Reflecting on what people have said to me over the years, there are three areas that stand out. I will explore these here but recognize that these are more specialist skills that take a lifetime to work on. Unlike some of the skills or steps presented earlier, which can be identified and practised quickly, these are ways of being that are related to the kind of person we are. Remember the list of qualities that counsellors aspire to, back in chapter 6? All of us need those qualities to be able to help other people, otherwise any skills we acquire will come across as some form of subtle control or manipulation.

1. Exploring silence

Most people don't like silence. In ordinary conversation a silence can seem awkward, with people not knowing what to say. When was the last time you spent any time in silence? It communicates absence, withdrawal, anger, impotence and powerlessness. Yet this need not be the case. Silence can be a gift, a time to stop and reflect, to allow thoughts and feelings to settle, and it can show a form of respect for another person in that we are not simply going to intrude. Silence offers both threat and opportunity. As an attentive listener the task is to find a helpful balance. That means we need to have discovered for ourselves if we are comfortable or uncomfortable with silence.

✳ Think for a moment; when was the last time you were silent for any length of time while with another person? How did that feel? Did it become so uncomfortable that you felt you had to speak? Even when we are comfortable with silence when we are with other people, they will often speak as they cannot bear it.

Working with silence is an important therapeutic skill used in all forms of counselling and psychotherapy. It can also be found in counselling skills and, as we shall now explore, in attentive listening. Heidi Levitt, a psychologist at the University of Memphis, has researched the use of silence in therapy and identified three types of silence: productive silence, neutral silence and obstructive silence. When silence emerges in our attentive listening it is helpful to keep these three categories in mind and ask ourselves the question: 'What kind of silence is this?'

Silence offers a deeply empathic connection when someone experiences overwhelming sadness, loss or pain. It offers the opportunity to show that we are not filling the uncomfortable emotional space with words but letting the person have the time and opportunity to reflect in their own mind. I once had a client who often lapsed into silences. At the end of the therapy they said in a quiet but clear voice, 'Thank you for all those times you let me be silent but did not leave me on my own.' Sometimes if another person is silent we have to work hard to stay with their experience, rather than getting bored or impatient and thinking 'I wish they would say something' or, 'Why don't they just get on with the conversation?'

The best preparation we can do is to become aware of how we use or avoid silence. Finding the time to sit in silence, focusing on breathing in and out for five minutes a day, can be hugely beneficial for you as well as for other people. It is amazing how this simple technique allows our mind to settle and our emotions to be recognized.

2. Exploring the unconscious

The word 'psycho-analytical' was not invented by Freud but by the British poet Samuel Taylor Coleridge who jotted in a notebook in 1805 that we need a 'strong imagination as well as an accurate psycho-analytical understanding' to understand an 'anonymous hidden life'. As examined earlier in the book, most people believe intuitively that there is an 'anonymous hidden life' that we more commonly call the unconscious. The commonest ways we experience the unconscious are through dreams and through a psychological mechanism called transference.

Transference happens when we transfer or displace thoughts, feelings, or wishes experienced with an important figure from our past onto a person in the present. So our past lives on in the present, and we experience other people as if they were that figure from our past, whether those relationships were positive or negative. While Freud, psychoanalysis, and psychodynamic therapies give a special place to transference as a therapeutic technique, it is a universal phenomenon that happens all the time inside and outside formal counselling contexts. We do it so often that it is unthinking, but each time we encounter a new person or a new experience we view it through the 'lens' of previous people and events. It is as if we are searching for a clue as to how to understand or respond, so that the threat of the new does not shock or overwhelm us.

All these recollections are stored in various regions of our brains (in a form of chemical memory) that can be reactivated in an instant through various dopamine pathways. The trigger may be someone listening to us in the same way as an old teacher once did, and so it automatically evokes the images, memories, feelings, emotions about this person. This becomes the 'lens' through which we see the person in the here and now. It is dominant in that moment and in our memory. This is a simplified version of events, as we have mixed feelings and emotions about most important people in our past. Yet in the present we can transfer these feelings, positive or negative, onto another person.

✳ Imagine the face of your favourite teacher from school. Recall a positive encounter you had with them. Listen again to the tone of voice and the way they responded to you. Remember their respectful attention that made you feel they really understood you. Now think about people in the present whom you feel very positive about. See if you have 'transferred' those early positive feelings without realizing this, seeing the person as if they were that teacher.

Let me illustrate this. I used to have a student who was always very prickly towards me and avoided me if she could. At some stage in the counselling training I revealed something about my past as an example, and afterwards she said she wanted to see me. She said that this story had really helped her, as she was able to see me as a person for the first time. She then shared that she had been abused by an uncle who had a grey beard (like me) and a soft Scottish accent (like me). Unknowingly, through this psychological process of transference, I had triggered feelings in her of wariness, avoidance and shame. She had been viewing me through the 'lens' of a male abusive authority figure based on her uncle. Yet now she was beginning to see me as the person I was, not the person she had seen me as.

Transference is always a helpful concept to have in mind when we are involved in attentive listening. There will be times when we hear accounts that don't really make sense, no matter how hard we listen or how well we use questions, exploring, clarifying, summarizing, paraphrasing, empathy, acceptance and a non-judgemental approach. The answer may lie in the fact that in listening to them we have triggered a transference response from the other person. This confuses them and complicates the process even more. Transference works both positively and negatively. While I gave an illustration of a negative transference response earlier, there can equally be positive transference responses. In another context a student had said they implicitly trusted me because I had a grey beard and blue eyes just like their grandfather. (I tried not to be too offended, despite thinking I was not anywhere near old enough to be their grandfather.) This illustrates that transference goes beyond the simple physical or age characteristics of a person. While the student knew I was not their grandfather they attributed to me qualities they experienced in their grandfather, but this happened without them initially knowing. They probably only discovered this because they were a student on a psychodynamic training course that got them to become aware of such issues.

3. A sense of presence

I suggested earlier that presence allows people to feel safe and to trust. This is an elusive but powerful part of engaging with other people. We don't always see it in ourselves, rather it is noted or observed in us by others. It is something that we all aspire to in our desire to be able to listen to other people. At the end of his life Rogers wrote about presence in his book, *A Way of Being*, that the very presence of the person can be healing for other people. Some have developed this idea to talk about a spiritual dimension of being with people, of awakening a 'divine spark', and as the ultimate expression of relational depth. Others link presence to the idea of sanctuary, evoking the expectation of safety and trust. As we attentively listen we can offer sanctuary and enable our very presence to profoundly help another person, not so much by what we do but by who we are. There are times when our being present with another human being enables us together to reach depths where no words need to be spoken. It can create a very powerful bond and be immensely healing for both. Such events are rare and cannot be manufactured. They are simply to be accepted as a gift that happens when two human beings meet at a profound level. This is not just the experience of counsellors after years of training; sometimes this can happen spontaneously through using the very listening skills we have explored in these last chapters.

We have now arrived at a good place to end our practical exploration of counselling. However, I hope it has whetted your appetite for even more. We have come a long way since I began by providing a brief definition of counselling as 'a relationship which helps make sense of life through being listened to, resolving feelings, clarifying thoughts, developing insight and promoting well-being'. Yet that was just the start, so what do I hope you have gained by reading this book and trying out the exercises?

First, I hope you will have acquired a greater understanding of what counselling is in its many forms – including how it works and who it helps. Central to this is the profound value of being human and the ability to enter into relationships with other people.

Second, you should know where counselling came from, as it evolved alongside psychoanalysis, psychotherapy, psychiatry and psychology and how each of these traditions contributes to emotional health and well-being. You can now see how counselling fits into a wider context, expressed through the values we aspire to and the ethical practices we engage in.

Third, you should now able to recognize what listening skills you already possess and to see how these can be developed in order to enhance the lives of other people.

At each stage there has been the recognition that it is us, as individuals, who are the greatest counselling 'tool' – our presence that we offer to other people. This act of attentive listening requires us to do a great deal of thinking and talking with others about whom and what we are.

Fourth, and finally, I hope you have discovered for the first time or rediscovered something unique about yourself as you have read these pages. Through that discovery you can see that you have the potential to offer something vital to other people that enhances their well-being. This may also be the first step in a journey that takes you further on in an exciting journey into professional training and accreditation as a therapist.

So I have high hopes for this book and I have high hopes for you as you read it, act on it and see new depths in yourself and your relationships.

Printed in Great Britain
by Amazon

26116046R00077